CW00507806

Mithra Omidvar

Sicily

and the Aeolian islands

Translated by Gill Round

50 selected walks on the coasts and in the mountains of Sicily
and on the Aeolian islands

With 81 colour photos,
50 walking maps to a scale of 1:50,000 and 1:75,000,
4 contextualising maps to a scale of 1:650,000 and 1:700,000
and 1 contextualising map to a scale of 1:2,300,000

ROTHER · MUNICH

Front cover:
Militello Rosmarino in Nebrodi.

Frontispiece (photo on page 2):
walks on the Aeolian islands: Lipari with Panarea and Strómboli.

All photos by the author.

Cartography:
walking maps to a scale of 1:50,000 and 1:75,000
© Bergverlag Rother GmbH, Munich (drawn by Kartographie Rolle, Holz-
kirchen), contextualising maps to a scale of 1:650,000, 1:700,000 and
1:2,300,000 © Freytag & Berndt, Vienna

Translated by Gill Round.

1st edition 2002
© Bergverlag Rother GmbH, Munich
ISBN 3-7633-4813-1

Distributed in Great Britain by Cordee, 3a De Montfort Street, Leicester
Great Britain LE1 7HD, www.cordee.co.uk
in USA by AlpenBooks, 3616 South Road, C-1, Mukilteo, WA 98275 USA,
www.alpenbooks.com

Preface

To hike in Sicily is to go on an adventure into a world of contrasts. It is the biggest Mediterranean island and, geologically speaking, is related to the Apennines, the Peloponnes, and also to North Africa. There's a huge difference between the climate at sea level and that in the mountains with altitudes ranging from 0 to 3300m. The geological and climatic components have a distinct influence on the island flora. There are over 3000 species of plants here, as many as on Sardinia, Corsica and Crete put together. They blossom directly next to the solidified lava like the flowers of paradise. Mountains constitute about one half of the island – hills and grassy plains the other. Between dessert ecology and that of frosty heights – everything is represented here. The ice regions of Mount Etna spew fire and glowing lava. Volcanic eruptions make the ground so fertile that for thousands of years people have been attracted by this good fortune and put up with the disadvantages. The geological location, the climate and the fertile soil have made Sicily a destination contested by many groups in spite of, or even because of, its peripheral situation. The result was an unusual political and cultural diversity. Thus an exciting transformation also began for nature: the Greeks brought with them the cultivation of olives and wine making. Citrus fruits and cleverly devised watering systems were introduced by the Saracens. The Normans and the Hohenstaufen dynasty encouraged the sciences. El Idrisi, the brilliant explorer and geographer at the court of Frederick II, worked on the first comprehensive cartographic study of Sicily. The Arabian country of the three headlands was based on the Greek Trinacria, the land of the three capes. Before that the native inhabitants symbolised the island by Triskéles, 'three legs', and Triquetra, 'the land of the triangle'. Everything points to mountains and to the three mountainous corners of Sicily. The idea of the 'three valleys of the foothills', Valli, is still used today to characterise the island. I have often wished for three legs myself as I have been exploring Sicily and found the helping hands of many Sicilian friends. For *me*, meeting the island's inhabitants has been the most rewarding and enjoyable experience in Sicily. This walking guide would never have come to fruition without the support of many mountain friends and people working in nature reserves, CAI branches and tourist offices. For the total exploration of the seemingly endless mountain landscape of Sicily, not even three legs would be enough – you would need a thousand! I hope you find the same helping hands as you go hiking in Sicily. If you identify anything different from the information given in these walk descriptions, please notify me via the publishers.

Autumn 2001

Mithra Omidvar

Contents

Tourist tips

Use of the guide

Corresponding to the three 'valleys of the foothills' (Val Démone, Val Mazara, Val di Noto) of ancient Trinacria, the guide is divided into three geological areas: the east, the west and the south-east. The Aeolian islands to the north of Sicily are dealt with as well. Mount Etna is assigned to the eastern section. Each area has a short introduction. The suggestions for walks consist of an information section, a short characterisation of the landscape you pass through and a description of the route. The individual maps to a scale of 1:50,000 and 1:75,000 are an integral part of the guide. They show the main route (continuous line) and alternative routes (broken line). All the selected mountains, locations, starting points and destinations can be found in the index at the back of the book. On the back cover and in the introduction to each area you will find a map giving the location of each walk.

At the Grotto di Cófano. The mountain of the same name is in the background (Walk 35).

Grades

Only a third of the walks described here are marked up to now, but not every marked walk is easy. A good sense of direction is important when walking in Sicily. On the other hand there are some walks described here which go along obvious paths, tracks and forest roads and do not present any problems with route-finding. Sections which require special care are mentioned in the individual walk descriptions. The grade might become harder depending on the time of year and weather conditions. Do not underestimate the fog when it occurs and the heat as well in the summer months which can make great demands on the hiker. To give you a clear sense of the grade, the walks in this guide are colour-coded as follows:

BLUE

These paths are either marked or the route-finding is easy. There is little danger involved and as they are only moderately steep, they are suitable for children and older people too.

RED

These walks are marked in places and are generally along mountain and narrow paths. They can be steep or exposed over short sections. Many of them are also quite long. They require good route-finding ability, sure-footedness and stamina and should only be undertaken by experienced hikers.

BLACK

These walks are hardly marked at all. They go mainly across country without paths and are often very long. Most of them require a high level of route-finding skills. Sections which are exposed or require some scrambling are specially mentioned in the walk description. These walks are only suitable for experienced, sure-footed and fit alpinists.

Dangers

Strong winds and sudden storms are not to be underestimated. Sometimes thick fog can make orientation difficult. The hot south wind, the Sirocco, can pose problems for those unused to the heat. Sulphur fumes on Etna, Vulcano and Strómboli can irritate the respiratory tracts. Check on the conditions of the volcanoes before embarking on walks in these areas.

Best season

You can go hiking in Sicily all year round. Very good conditions for hiking are between December and February. The ridge areas from 1000m upwards can be covered in snow or ice at this time of year and then you will need winter gear to venture up Etna. Spring and autumn are unreservedly good months for hiking. You have to cope with the considerable heat in summer, so choose your walk according to its length and steepness.

Equipment

Sturdy footwear with good soles, hard-wearing trousers, protection against rain, cold winds and sun, as well as food (especially enough fluids) are essentials on every walk. It's highly recommended that you take a compass and altitude measure with you on hikes which are not on paths. (Small secateurs, too, often prove useful on many of the walks which can become overgrown in a few weeks.)

Maps

Italian IGM maps (Istituto Geografico Militare) to a scale of 1:25,000 and 1:50,000 are available in Sicily, but unfortunately they are no longer up-to-date (up to 40 years old!). For Etna national park you can obtain a map to the scale of 1:50,000 from the Touring Club Italia. The Madonie park administration has also published recently a walking map of the area to the same scale. Unfortunately neither is on the market but you can get hold of one from the park authorities.

Access

The good bus network does not necessarily reach all starting points on the island. There is no service out of season to many places or only one with a limited service. Taxis, when available are expensive.
Hitch-hiking is not really an option since the locals hardly ever stop to give you a lift. Hotels sometimes offer a taxi service, but it's frequently necessary to hire your own car.

Walking times

The information only refers to the real walking time – without breaks and photo opportunities. To help you with your planning you will find information about the time for each stage, total walking time and variation in height.

Stops and accommodation

On Mount Etna there are some staffed huts and many self-catering ones. The latter can only be used if accompanied by local guides or by prior arrangement. The few staffed huts in the Madonie region can be reached by car, or otherwise it's the same procedure as on Etna. Staffed huts like in the Alps are non-existent. It's recommended that you get hold of a list of accommodation (including hotels, *agriturismo* establishments etc.) before traveling (see p. 16).
For walks lasting more than a day you will need a tent or a bivouac. The route of the long distance path 'Sentiero Italia' is chosen so that you can find accommodation at the end of each stage. In every small village there's at least a bar and a pizzeria and in the more popular villages the locals also rent out rooms. In larger villages you'll always find a *locanda* (simple guest

house). There's a big choice of restaurants and hotels in the more tourist developed areas. The same is true of campsites.

Agriturismo

Agriturismo is equivalent to the 'farm holiday' idea, but because of the tax advantages some of this type of accommodation is not all that it seems. Most of the establishments only offer a restaurant service, many are only open at the weekend and only a few are truly agricultural establishments. Information can be obtained from, amongst other places: Agriturist Sicilia, Via Alessio Giovanni, 14, I-90144 Palermo, tel: 091346046, e-mail: agriturist@mcsystem.it.

Nature and the environment

A Sicilian's first love is the forest, where coolness is found in summer, and mushrooms, wild boar and whatever else nature has to offer the local hunter and collector. And yet nowhere else is there as much exploitation of nature. Nowhere are the consequences longer lasting than on this sensitive island

In the mountains, agriculture is for many only a secondary occupation.

The Madonie wild peonies.

province of Sicily. Limestone terrain and water shortage in the long hot summers make this country susceptible to environmental damage. Therefore please help: be sparing with the water, do not leave any rubbish behind or throw cigarette ends down in the countryside and do not light open fires (acute risk of forest fire!). Report any suspicious fires to SOS Boschi, tel: 1515.

Gates and fences

You will frequently find boundary and field fences, and gates on a Sicilian walk. Sometimes they cut off extremely important routes, even marked ones, and you often have to go looking for a gap, or laboriously climb over the fence. It's okay to do that. When opening closed gates, always remember to close them again behind you. Shepherds and landowners will be grateful to you.

Paths and waymarkers

Paths are being marked systematically and at great expense in Sicily. Instead of repairing old paths, they are building new roads. The result is erosion. They are also gathering experience about what type and colour waymarkers to use. Be patient when you are looking despairingly for a sign: it's yellowish-green, in Sicily's spring colours, so that it looks 'environmentally friendly'. And do not get cross if the farmer has taken a waymarker to use in his vineyard. Path maintenance is unknown here in the countryside!

Walking in Sicily

Geography

With a surface area of 25,708 sq. km, Sicily is the largest of the Mediterranean islands and is extraordinarily varied with altitudes of almost 2000m (Madonie) and over 3000m (Etna). Only 3km separate the island from the Italian mainland. After the straits of Messina the Apennines reappear in a long chain and determine the mountainous composition of north-eastern Sicily. This chain is called Appennino Sículo which is subdivided into the Peloritani near Messina, the Nebrodi near Capo d'Orlando and the Madonie near Cefalù. The huge cleft of the Himera between Cefalù and Tèrmini Imerese separates the east from the west, followed by the individual ranges of the western Sicilian mountains and south of them, Monti Sicani. The heart of Sicily, the central Sicilian basin, Monti Erei, stretches between Enna and Gela to the south. The limestone plateau of the Hyblaean mountains lies in the south, near Noto and Syrakus. Sicily has been divided into three valley regions since classical antiquity: Val Démone in the east, Val di Mazara in the west and Val di Noto in the south. Etna lies on a magmatic crack which stretches from Vesuvius across the Aeolian islands to Panteleria in the south-west. As an independent massif, it characterises definitively the eastern Sicilian landscape.

Flora and fauna

The vast expanse of Sicily and the large variations in height, as well as the geological and climatic diversity, encourage rich plant life. The stands of forest have been severely decimated by the constant exploitation of natural spaces. There are forests covering vast areas on Mount Etna, in the Nebrodi, on the northern slopes of the Madonie and in Ficuzza near Palermo. Beech, downy cork, and holm oak, as well as ash are indigenous. Intensive reforestation with 'imported' pines and eucalyptus trees is intended to extend the 'green lungs' of nature and thereby reinforce the slopes. But eucalyptus tends to suck dry the areas of dampness. The Manna ash grows in the Madonie. Its nectar was once tapped by whole family communities and then marketed. There are also a few examples of the endemic

Flowers for the procession.

Nebrodi fir (*Abies nebrodiensis*) which have survived from the tertiary period and a great number of large hollies (*Ilex aquifolium*) from the Ice Age. The evergreen macchia with cistus, *Pistacia lentricus*, tree heather, strawberry trees etc. covers wide areas of the mountain slopes and coasts. The island is in flower almost all year round. Blossoming starts on the coasts in winter and stretches up the foothills in spring. In summer and autumn blossom covers the high mountain areas before descending again.

The colours of Sicily are green and yellow: yellow oxalis, wild fennel, gorse, Ferula, spurge, Inula, *Dihrichia viscosa* etc. Wild peonies grow white and red in the shady forests. Botany lovers are delighted to find cyclamen, star anemones, and numerous orchids, and amongst them rare types of Ophrys.

Environmental organisations are trying bit by bit to protect animals living in the wild from further extinction. Wild boar, wild cats, martens, foxes, weasels, the common dormouse and other even smaller mammals were able to escape extinction. There's only an occasional white-headed vulture

in western Sicily, but the golden eagle has returned to the Nebrodi and the Madonie. You will also find the short-toed eagle, the common bussard, the osprey and peregrine falcon and, in the Aeolian islands, the Eleonora falcon. Since the strict ban on setting nets has been imposed, numerous other species of birds are able to fly freely and undisturbed. And we must not forget the wild horses of S. Fratello, an endemic breed, whose forerunners date from the Arabian era in Sicily.

The 'eternal' colours of Sicily.

Nature parks and nature reserves
There are no national parks in Sicily. The protected areas are either regional, provincial or municipal parks. The first regional park, Parco dell'Etna, originated in 1987 and covers 58,000 hectares. Then followed Parco delle Madonie in 1989, with almost 40,000 hectares, and dei Nebrodi in 1993, with over 85,000 hectares. Other protected areas are the nature reserves which Sicily has put into the hands of various environmental organisations, like for example, WWF, Legambiente, CAI (Italian Alpine Club) etc. The Riserva Naturale Vendicari, Isola di Lampedusa, Grotta di Santa Ninfa and Monte Conca are some of these. The nature reserve of Lo Zingaro was

The western side of Etna with the lava flow from October 1999.

set up in 1980 at a mass rally, and became the first officially protected area in Sicily. The above organisations were largely responsible for this.

The 'Sentiero Italia' and other long distance walks

About 600km of the 6000km Italian long distance path ‚'Sentiero Italia', are on Sicilian territory. The Italian Alpine Club in Sicily has already tested the path twice, in 1995 and 1999, and yet the path is still not completely marked. (In the provinces of Palermo and Syrakus, as well as on Mount Etna, there are some waymarkers on the path, but they are not always marked as 'Sentiero Italia'.) You will not find any overnight accommodation, nor are there maps or walking guides. Starting points and destinations are either Messina in the east or Erice in the west. There are 36 day stages through Sicily's mountain areas: through the Peloritani, right round Etna, across the Nebrodi and the Madonie, through the west Sicilian mountains in the provinces of Palermo and Trápani as far as Rocca Erice. An alternative to this trek includes a crossing of the Hyblaean limestone plateau as far as Etna and consists of a further 12 stages.

Shorter long distance walks are possible in almost all of the mountain regions. An excellent walk is from hut to hut round Etna and you can expect this to take about a week. The park authorities have put up waymarkers along a network of paths in the Madonie on an extensive scale. Several routes can be linked with one another here.

Information and addresses

Getting there
You can travel by ferry from Civitavecchia, La Spezia, Livorno and Genoa to Palermo. There's also a ferry twice a week from Naples via the Aeolian islands to Milazzo, and a regular ferry from Villa S. Giovanni in Calabria to Messina. Scheduled flights to Palermo and Catania usually go via the Italian mainland and mainly during the high season there are charter flights on offer.

Camping
There are just under 100 campsites and information and addresses can be obtained from the tourist offices or E.N.I.T. Otherwise nearly all the road maps have a list.

Climate
You will notice a climate change even in Sicily. Usually it is very hot from July to September (up to over 40 °C). Spring and autumn are pleasantly warm months and winter is relatively mild. There can be frequent showers in November.

INFORMATION

Italian State Tourist Board E.N.I.T.:
- E.N.I.T., Level 26, 44 Market Street NSW, 2000 Sidney, Australia, tel. (0061) 2 92621666
- E.N.I.T., 175 Bloor Street, Suite 907, South Tower, M4W3R8 Toronto (Ontario), Canada, tel. +1 (416) 9254882
- E.N.I.T., 1 Princes Street, W1R2AY London, Great Britain, tel. (0044) 20 74081254
- E.N.I.T., 630, Fifth Avenue, Suite 1565, 10111 New York, USA, tel. +1 (212) 2454822

In Sicily:
- Assessorato Regionale del Turismo, Via Emmanuele Notarbartolo 9, I-90141 Palermo, tel. 0916961111

Tourist offices in the provinces (APT):
- Agrigento, tel. 092226926
- Catania, tel. 095310888
- Messina, tel. 090675356
- Palermo, tel. 091586122
- Syrakus, tel. 093167607
- Trápani, tel. 093327273
- Aeolian islands, tel. 0909880095

Nature park administrations:
- Parco dell'Etna, tel. 095914588
- Parco dei Nebrodi, tel. 0921333211
- Parco delle Madonie, tel. 0921644011

Cefalà Diana and the Calamagnia mountains.

Emergency

Mountain rescue, see below   Police (Carabinieri) 112
SOS Boschi 1515   Breakdown (Soccorso Stradale/ACI) 116

Hiking clubs

The CAI (Club Alpino Italiano) of Sicily has its main office in Messina. Other branches are to be found in some of the provincial towns. The president with an address for all enquiries is Gianni Mento: CAI Sicilia, Via Natóli, 26, I-98100 Messina, tel: 0906510126 or 3479616387 (mobile), fax: 090694669; CAI, Catania, tel: 0957153515 or 3474111632 (mobile); CAI, Syrakus, tel: 093164751; CAI, Petralia, tel: 0921641028; CAI, Palermo (the best organised and most active branch with an extensive programme for members, Toti Fresta, is always open to enquiries), tel. and fax: 091329407; CAS (Club Alpino Siciliano), independent from CAI, tel: 091581323.

Mountain rescue (Corpo Nazionale Soccorso Alpino e Speleologico)

There still isn't a central mountain rescue service in Sicily. The section of the 'Guardia Finanza' in the province of Catania has set up a mountain rescue department in Nicolosi at Etna. Tel: 117, and ask for Soccorso Alpino

Nicolosi. Members of the mountain rescue in Palermo are also at your disposal: V. Biancone (team leader) tel: 0916702156 and 360407675 (mobile); G. Maurici (assistant manager) tel: 091514712 and 360405457 (mobile); office, tel: 0916740237.

National holidays

1st January, 6th January, Easter, 25th April, 1st May, 15th August, 1st November, 8th, 25th and 26th December.
There are also local festivals when the banks, shops etc. are closed.

Sport

Sicily is a paradise for all water sports, and horse-riding and cycling are gaining popularity. Guided tours and trips through caves, gorges, mountains, on the coast and on the sea are organised amongst others by:

Hiking and natural history tours: Green Ecogest: tours throughout Sicily. tel: 3470977098 (mobile); fax 091336475, e-mail: greenecogest@hotmail.com; Artemisia: hiking in Palermo and surrounding area, e-mail: artemisianet@katamail.com;

Riserva Naturale Saline di Trápani: to the salt deposits in the west, tel. and fax: 0923867700, e-mail: wwf.rnotp@male.cinet.it;

Mare Terra: alternative holidays amidst sun, water and fire, http://web.tiscalinet.it/sicilia_mareeterra/;

Cooperativa 'Il Sentiero': guided hikes on Lipari and Vulcano, tel: 3384793064 (mobile), e-mail: sentiero@netnet.it.

Watersport: Euroyachting Club: sailing, tel. and fax: 091455851, e-mail: alberie@tin.it; Mare Nostrum: diving, tel. and fax: 091211584.

Cycling: Siciclando, one-day and multi-day tours, tel: 3286916989 or 3472900918 (both mobile), e-mail: info@siciclando.com.

Educational biological tours: Legambiente Nebrodi: information and educational tours in Nebrodi national park, tel: 0941955157.

Telephone

The code for Sicily (Italy) is 0039, but you have to dial the 0 of the local dialing code as well! With mobile numbers do not dial the 0, even when you're on the island. In Italy you have to use the local dialling code even when making local calls!

Theft

There are some precautionary measures to help you enjoy a relaxing holiday in Sicily: do not leave anything valuable in the car. Remove anything worth stealing from the seats and always lock the boot.

While there is hardly any danger in the mountains and mountain villages, you need to be on your toes in towns and not only because of the traffic.

Take great care in the big hotels too. Going to the police has little effect, so be sure to take evidence of your insurance with you.

Transport
There's a well organised bus network all over the island which runs services to even the smallest villages at least once a day. Overland buses travel punctually and quickly and connect the cities with one another, and with the airports, ferry ports and stations. The main train lines are Messina – Palermo and Messina – Catania – Syrakus – Agrigent. For all local services you need time and patience.

Educational tours on M. Conca (Walk 37).

The east

What would Sicily be without **Etna**? There can be no better answer than the view across the bay from Naxos to the biggest volcano in Europe: in its place there would be an enormous chasm full of water from the Greek theatre in Taormina as far as the cathedral of Catania. And that's what it was like a million years ago. Masses of lava poured into the depths of the sea and over a 600,000 year long and constant period of activity, the collision of the continents lifted up the volcano. It reaches a massive height of 3300m, covers an area of 1750 sq. km, has a base circumference of 212km, a diameter of 42km, a volume of 500 cubic km, the temperaure in the magma oven is 1221 °C, the pressure of 1392 atmospheres … When it all gets too much, Etna lets off a bit of steam from time to time. And that's how its roughly 400 secondary craters have originated and at least as many vents. It is one of the 'less dangerous' volcanoes, although it has already inundated Catania with lava eleven times. Actually from a distance it looks peaceful and suspended, hovering above the luxuriant orchards and fields of its surroundings. The balanced pH value of its lava quickly produces solidified rivers of lava and fertile soil. All that, combined with the altitude and the different climatic zones, attracts biological expeditions to the smoking giant, as exciting as they are volcanological. Even a tour round its gigantic cone, either on the **Circumetnea** narrow-gauge railway or by car, reveals its many facets. The **Simento** river in the south and the **Alcántara** in the north wash round it and the Ionian sea laps its eastern coast. The Etna villages are fearlessly lined up in a chain around it: Nicolosi, Adrano, Bronte, Randazzo, Linguaglossa and others. There's hardly a single walk on the island which does not have a view of Etna from some point. The most attractive walk is, without doubt, from Taormina and has made Sicily famous.

Mount Etna is the youngest mountain in Sicily while the **Peloritani**, close by in the north-east, form the oldest mountain range on the island. Its crystalline rock corresponds to the composition of the Aspromonte in Calabria. The shape of the landscape is also very similar. Characteristic are the *fiumare*, enormously broad, deeply riven valleys where the rivers wash down the unstable slate in the rainy period and cause devastation to many places. You can experience the bizarre, fissured landscape of the Peloritani on the walk along the 'Sentiero Girasi' (Walk 6) where the *'strada militare'* originated in the time of Mussolini. It runs 40km from the coast through the mountains. As a relic of the second world war it is only passable in places. Driving on the coastal road SS 113 from **Messina** to **Villafranca Sicilia** is a must. In May and June you can see the special boats for catching swordfish cruising back and forth in the **Stretto di Messina**. The tall masts and the long bows are quite striking. The slender limestone rock of **Rocca di Novara** stands out again and again like a waymarker, whether viewed from along the coast, the Aeolian islands or the island's interior. You should linger in the small valleys and along the narrow mountain roads between **Novara** and **Montalbano**. At the tiny village of **S. Cono** you can see across **Tripi** and Novara to the Rocca and southwards to the smoking Etna. Every year in Montalbano, in the forests of **Malabotta** and in **Tindari**, you become aware of the devoutness of the local people. Thousands of pilgrims on foot, sometimes all the way from their home village, come to honour the Black Madonna of Tindari. This pilgrim's way also runs to some extent along the border between Peloritani and **Nebrodi**. But the landscapes merge easily. Many valleys between Tindari and **S. Ágata di Militello**, some of them *fiumare*, cut deep into the landscape. Small villages in safe locations decorate the peaks on the ridge which drops down to the sea. Excursions from

Peloritani and the waymarker Rocca die Novara; Tripi in the foreground.

Pastures in the limestone hollows of the Madonie.

Capo d'Orlando to the forests of Nebrodi are always a delight and deeply satisfying. Genuine Sicilian food can be sampled in the small villages, as well as at **Portella Femmina Morta** in the 'Villa Miraglia' guest house. From here you can undertake a bumpy journey and then a hike to the **Biviere di Cesaro**. The biotope lies at the foot of **Monte Soro**, with 1847m the highest mountain in the Nebrodi. The heart of this landscape is a softly undulating sandstone mountain of arkosic sandstone, clay and sedimentary deposit. The link road from **Cesaró** via **Troina**, **Cerami** and **Nicosia** to **Sperlinga** runs parallel to the densely forested main ridge. The intensively farmed pasture and cornfields extend to the south of this. The wonderful scenery is an unforgettable experience if you look from the hills of M. Sambughetti to Etna. Fortresses were built on the old mountain road Messina – Palermo by the Normans in the 11th century and inhabited by immigrants from the mainland. The fortress of Sperlinga was skilfully cut into the rocks – just like the dwellings of local people. The dense **forest of Sperlinga** dates from this feudal era. S. Stefan di Camastra lies on the coast with its century old ceramic tradition. In the 15th century almost all families were still involved with the production of clay pots. Today numerous shops have set up in business along the main highway. Amongst the surplus of wares you will still find ancient motifs whose antique originals are to be seen in the museums. Just to the west of S. Stefan you cross over **Fiume Tusa** and enter the **Parco delle Madonie**. It's well worth going up to Pollina and walking through the narrow streets to the viewing terrace. There's a wide and impressive view from here of the Madonie with the highest elevations of the massif. An almost 2000m limestone mass rises up directly out of the sea at a distance of less than 40km. When walking in the heart of the Madonie there are fossils and petrified molluscs to be found at the side of the path. The two closely neighbouring mountain areas of Nebrodi and Madonie are strikingly different. Dramatic rocky landscapes and Mediterranean fragrances predominate here, as well as sheep rearing and characteristically pastoral traditions. The villages occupy the most beautiful locations on the slopes all around the massif, like **Castelbuono** at the foot of the holm oak forests, the 'second residence' of the aristocratic Ventimiglia family, which had its seat in **Geraci Sículo**. Geraci is reached through extensive cork oak forests. The village of **Gangi** 'embraces' the pyramid of the mountain on which it settled. It's a very picturesque scene looking from **Petralia Soprana** with Etna in the background. The two Petralie villages, like most of the Madonie villages, were founded by feudal barons for the cultivation and protection of territory. The pretty village of Petralia Soprana spreads along the crest of a mountain ridge whereas **Petralia Sottana** originated at a later date further below and is now the central town of Madonie. This is where the large hospital for the whole area is being built. The infrastructure of the town received support from the land registry and other important government centres, eg. Madonie nature park authorities. With much élan, young people have set up a museum of local art where you can learn about the customs and festivals in the area. The festival celebrated in honour of the patron saint, San Calógero, on the 18th June, is by far the most important. In **Isnello** at the beginning of September there's a two day festival for the patron saint of S. Nicola di Bari village. The limestone grottoes of **Gratteri**, the natural history museum in **Polizzi Generosa** and many other attractions invite you to linger a while longer.

Cefalù and the Madonie are usually mentioned in one breath. In local legend, a storm and the power struggle of King Roger II are said to have resulted in the building of the wonderful Norman cathedral and the town around it. On an easy walk to the castle mountain you will discover relics from the 9th century BC, but also a delightful coastal landscape. The eastern foothills, **Val Démone**, come to an end eventually at Fiume Imera.

1   Etna: Bocca Nuova, 3260m

Looking into the interior of the earth

Piccolo Rifugio – Cisternazza – Torre del Filosofo – Bocca Nuova – Torre del Filosofo – Cisternazza – Rifugio Sapienza

Locations: Zafferana, Nicolosi.
Starting point: Piccolo Rifugio, 2550m. Access the volcano in the direction of

'Etna Sud', park at the Rifo. Sapienza, 1927m. By jeep to the mountain station, at the moment as far as Piccolo Rifo.

Walking times: Piccolo Rifo. – Torre del Filosofo 1¼ hrs., T. d. Filosofo – Bocca Nuova 1½ hrs., return 1 hr., T. d. Filosofo – Cisternazza ¾ hr., Cisternazza – Montagnola south ½ hr., ash slope – Etna road ½ hr., Etna road – Rifo. Sapienza ¼ hr.; total time 5¾ hrs.

Ascent: 710m in ascent, 1400m in descent.

Grade: alternating broad and obvious hiking paths, narrow paths and tracks; no waymarkers. Sometimes difficult over ash, solidified lava and cinders. High standard of fitness as well as a good sense of direction essential due to the high altitude. This walk should only be undertaken during clear visibility!

Food and accommodation: a big selection from Zafferana and Nicolosi on the way to the starting point. Bars, restaurants and Rifo. Sapienza at the cable-car station, CAI hut.

NB: volcanic eruptions can alter the route. The eruption of summer 2001 once again destroyed the cable railway. The road to Torre del Filosofo still needs to be cleared. If you do not want any help with the ascent, you can walk up the jeep road (reckon on about 1 hr. extra).

Encountering an active volcano at close proximity is an awesome experience for all of the senses. The ascent, however, is dependent on its activities. So if you should find a barrier across the path up to the summit crater, there's enough room on Etna's southern slopes for other very interesting geology and volcanology expeditions.

At present the jeep road ends just above the Piccolo Rifugio which was flattened by massive lava flows in July 2001 together with the cable railway.

Above it rises Montagnola, which was created by an eruption in 1763. Ski lifts go up to its summit. About 200m to the left of it you can see the still un-officially named Montagnola II, also known as 'Tazief' after the French vol-canologist Haroun Tazief, which originated on 25.7.2001. This new second-ary crater is one of four vents which Etna has recently produced along the north-south line between the south-east crater (below the summit) and the Etna road (above the Silvestri crater).

Looking down into the Valle del Bove as you descend the ridge. The towns of Giarre and Riposto lie on the coast.

Cross the solidified lava stream above **Piccolo Rifo.** to the east and then, at the foot of Montagnola, go along the lava outflow crack, up between bombs and clinkers of the 'Tazief' to the col of the two secondary craters. Go across other lava fields on the left, as far as you can in the upper area, to soon reach some fields of ash. Once you've arrived above a crater in the ground, go right, gently uphill to the east, to experience a real spectacle at the rim of the valley. This viewpoint is called **Cisternazza** and has a fantastic view into the Valle del Bove and over to the Cyclopean coast. This deeply-cut valley, once fertile pasture-land (*bove* = ox), was created through an explosion. Now turn to the north towards the summit. Below it lie the ruins of Rifo. Torre del Filosofo and lower down the 'Hornitos' at another recent outflow point. Head for the most prominent one and climb up to it on fields of ash. The rather laborious climb to the top starts just to the right of this *hornito*. From the top you can look down into the chasm. At the back of it, first of all descend and then continue climbing up across the ash to the **Torre del Filosofo**. The distant view across the layers of lava and the twin craters you've left behind is stunning. The summit craters lie ahead. At this point you come to some lava dating from 1999. From the ruins go across to the left, the west, and reach a broad path along which you ascend to the right. This path gets gradually narrower and meanders up to the summit, but you can hardly make out the path at the end. You also come to the edge of the **Bocca Nuova** (be careful!). Created in 1968, it belongs to the central crater together with the somewhat higher 'Voragine Centrale'. With the north-eastern and south-eastern crater they form the summit of Etna. With a favourable wind the sulphur clouds allow you a view down into the deep crater. Magma and gases come up out of the belly of the earth with enormous pressure and the corresponding background noises.

Descend along the same path, cross the slope past **Cisternazza** to the col, go down the ash to the edge of the Valle del Bove and to the south over a last lava flow on the ridge. Cross the eastern slopes of Montagnola and Canalone della Montagnola, a gully which drops down deeply to the left. Keeping at the same height (about 2500m) and on an obvious path, make a leisurely descent to the south side of Montagnola. On the right in the west you look across a wide, fissured lava landscape to the valley station at the Rifo. Sapienza. The secondary craters of Silvestri are in the foreground. There now follows a soft ash track which runs down in a straight line from Montagnola southwards to the Etna road. It's a fast descent on the increasingly narrow path which is later covered in ash. There's a pine wood on the left. You reach the road between an iron gate, left, and a car park, right (1860m). From here go right, past the Silvestri craters to the **Rifo. Sapienza**.

Flowing lava is piled up and solidifies into hornitos.

2 Etna: Pizzi Deneri, 2847m

A glimpse into Etna's past

Rifugio Citelli – Serra delle Concazze – Rocca della Valle – Pizzi Deneri – Monte Frumento – Rifugio Citelli

Locations: Linguaglossa and Fornazzo.
Starting point: Rifo. Citelli, 1746m. The northern Etna mountain road goes up near Linguaglossa and Fornazzo. Turn off to the Rifo. Citelli, park at the end of the road at the hut.
Walking times: Rifo. Citelli – Serra delle Concazze 1¾ hrs., Serra delle Concazze – Rocca della Valle 1 hr., Rocca della Valle – P. Deneri ½ hr., P. Deneri – Rifo. Citelli 2¼ hrs.; total time 5½ hrs.
Ascent: 1000m.
Grade: ash, the altitude and walking across terrain with no paths make the conditions difficult. Only white and red waymarkers at the start. Good route-find-

ing ability and fitness are essential.
Food and accommodation: Rifo. Citelli (CAI hut), rooms and bunkhouse. Hotels at Piano Provenzana.
Alternative: from the observatory there's a track going to a cross-road. Turn left and reach the summit craters in 1½ hrs. From Bocca Nuova, 3260m, in clear visibility and a favourable wind, you can climb up left to the highest point, Bocca Subterminale, 3330m. Return: possible to take a short-cut across ash and lava back to the observatory. This ascent is only recommended in perfect weather, during moderate volcanic activity and with a favourable wind (sulphur fumes).

From a distance Etna looks like a uniformly shaped cone. But on closer inspection with it has many facets. The walk to the Pizzi Deneri gives you a fabulous view of the summit craters, Valle del Leone and Valle del Bove. The craggy Valle del Bove was once fertile pasture-land, and it's possible that it was created by an enormous explosion.

From the **Rifugio Citelli** you can see up to the ridge and a gully leads down from a conspicuous notch. Your path leads up to the left of this: descend along the tarmac road, leave the road on the right hand bend and ascend up into the wood. Gaining height along tracks of ash you can see M. Frumento delle Concazze on your right. Reach the broad ridge, **Serra delle**

Descending the ash track to the side crater of M. Frumento.

Concazze, on 2350m just below the notch you could see earlier. The sea with the Cyclopean coast comes into view and you look down into the huge Valle del Bove. Two secondary craters are just ahead of you. Below on the left, Monte Simone and on the right, Monte Rittmann. The path goes up steeply to the right along the ridge to **Rocca della Valle**. The walk is easier from here onwards. During the next ½ hr. you pass several elevations on the ridge. The **Pizzi Deneri** are completely covered with surveying stations from the Catania Volcanological Institute. From the first peak you can see the ash path on the right which you will be descending. There's a good view of M. Frumento from the second elevation and the view into the Alcantara valley is very impressive from here too. Almost half of Sicily, from the Ionian coast westwards, is stretched out below you. The 500m higher summit craters, north-east, central and south-east craters, block the view to the south. Eventually the volcanological observatory is visible from the highest point. Piano Provenzano lies below with the skiing area of Etna-north. Piano delle Concazze lies on the left and the Valle del Leone.

Go back to the first of the Pizzi Deneri for the descent, descend the ash gully down to **Monte Frumento** and above this meet a path which you follow across two small valleys to the east and to the road which brings you to the **Rifugio Citelli**.

3 Etna: Monti Sartorius, 1770m

A nature trail on Mount Etna

Barrier – shepherds' hut – Monti Sartorius – barrier

Locations: see Walk 2.
Starting point: barrier on the path to M. Sartorius, 1667m. Access as in Walk 2, but park on the right, 1km from the turn-off, in the latitude of a barrier (sign 'Monti Sartorius, Sentiero Natura').
Walking times: barrier – stone house 1 hr., stone house – col on M. Sartorius ½ hr., col – barrier ¼ hr.; total time 1¾ hrs.
Ascent: 150m.
Grade: an easy walk on marked paths, but you should try to take longer than the time specified! A short section over lava rock is without paths.
Food and accommodation: see Walk 2.

The high altitude and the enormous bulk give Etna its scenic diversity. Of the greatest scientific interest, it has attracted researchers from all over the world. Sartorius, the cartographer from Waltershausen, recorded the most important eruptions of Etna. He climbed the volcano during the eruption in November 1842 and jumped for joy on the streams of flowing lava. He surfed the lava until the soles of his shoes became too hot. In 1856 he gave a lecture on this and other Etna activities at the conference of German naturalists in Vienna. The secondary craters on this walk were named after him.

The nature trail starts behind the **barrier**. Each observation point (Punto di Osservazione, PO) is marked. Wooden posts with yellow paint mark the route. Right from the start you can see the Pizzi Deneri above to the left and one of Etna's biggest secondary craters, Monte Frumento delle Concazze, through the forest. On the right look over to the slopes of Monti Sartorius which is where you will return.

Go straight on through a beautiful birchwood which is interspersed with black pines and the endemic Etna gorse (*Genista aetnensis*). The walk leads over soft ash and past 'bombs'. These large rocks are lumps of lava which were thrown out during an eruption and then solidified in the air. They have different shapes and surfaces depending on the rotation and composition. Below Monte Frumento can be found the typical, prickly Astragalus cushion. After about ¾ hr. walking you come to a derelict **stone house** (*ovile*) with a water trough. Leave the broad path here to go to the right. Beyond the little house in the forest there's a large rock of lava growing out of the birch trees (waymarker). The rock forms a stark colour contrast to the delicate plants, like, for example, *Festuca pratensis* and *Poa alpina*. The now narrow path winds its way for about 10 mins. between birch trees, past waymarker posts, down through a little valley (gully). Be careful: do not descend too far!

Shortly after waymarker No. 4 you come to a platform with the next post. You have to climb up here to the right. Once on the ridge go slightly to the right (south). You find yourself standing in a clearing on the north side of Monti Sartorius, which you now walk round. Going straight on you meet the lava flow from 1865. Another volcanic cone is ahead. On the right of this you see a col which you head towards. The path there leads right across the lava flow. For over a century there has only been sparse vegetation here. The lava decomposes faster or slower according to the acid or base content. On the col you go up to the edge of the left hand cone from where you can see Rocca di Novara and the sea behind with the Aeolian islands.

Back on the col, descend to the broad path and return left to the starting point at the **barrier**. There you see the Rifo. Citelli opposite on a hill.

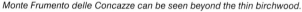

Monte Frumento delle Concazze can be seen beyond the thin birchwood.

4 Etna: Monte Nuovo, 1670m

The volcano of volcanoes

Casa Forestale Piano dei Grilli – Monte Rúvolo – Monte Lepre – Monte Nuovo

Location: Bronte, west of Etna.
Starting point: Casa Forestale Piano dei Grilli, 1160m. On the way to Randazzo, at the northern end of Bronte right (sign 'Ristorante Etrusca'). Turn right after 7km at a junction (bar) and between fields of lava continue along a basalt paved road as far as the wooden gate of Etna nature park.
Walking times: car park – lava from 1763 ¾ hr., lava – pine forest 1 hr., summit –

ascent ½ hr., return 2 hrs.; total time 4¼ hrs.
Ascent: 510m.
Grade: broad path throughout, marked with signs, except the last section up to M. Nuovo which is without paths and over lava and ash.
Food and accommodation: bars, restaurant, hotel in Bronte.

The thin earth crust on Etna causes the magma chamber to rise up to 3180m above sea level. The pressure of the gases is expelled partly through the main chimney, partly through the cracks on the steep slopes. Over 400 secondary craters of Etna, also called side, parasitic or adventive craters, are also vents for the excess pressure.

M. Nuovo, M. Rúvolo, M. Minardo, three of the numerous side craters near Bronte.

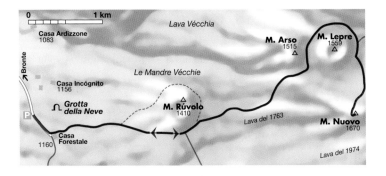

You begin the walk behind the wooden gate along the broad forest road. It leads for ¼ hr. towards M. Rúvolo via Piano delle Ginestre. Go right at a fork, and ¼ hr. after that carry straight on at the next turn-off. You meet another (signed) turn-off amongst tree-high Etna gorse (*Genista aetnensis*). Right goes to Monti Tre Frati. Straight on, at **M. Rúvolo** and past a left hand turn-off, you come out of the forest and find yourself at **the lava flow of 1763**. Etna rises steeply up ahead. The black lava of 1999 is easily recognisable on its steep flanks. M. Nuovo lies below, dark and black, and stands out well from the other overgrown side craters. To the left of it stands M. Mezzaluna, the 'half moon' and in between them Monte Rosso – true to its name with the red soil.

Your route goes between **M. Arso** and **M. Lepre**, then through a small wood. Climb uphill to the right around M. Lepre. Past some huge oak trees you reach a cross path. Left goes to M. Egitto and M. Scavo, but you turn right and stay on the broad path below enormous pine trees until you reach a conspicuous left-hand bend (sign: 'M. Nuovo'). Here you leave the main path to the right. Through the wood first head towards the black slopes of M. Nuovo. Leave the path to the right shortly before it swings to the left. On open ground you see a col opposite which you head towards, without paths, over clinkers and ash. It's worth climbing up from the col to the left crater of **M. Nuovo**: first to the left, then down into a hollow and finally along well-trodden tracks curving round left up to the highest point. At first your view to the west is of the somewhat lower cone ahead, but then you can see the path as far as Piana delle Ginestre and the town of Bronte surrounded by pistachio groves with the Monti Nebrodi chain of mountains rising above.

Return the same way.

5 Monte Scuderi, 1253m

The incomparable viewpoint of the Cyclopean coast

Itàla – Sorgente Seddiri – Monte Scuderi – Sorgente Seddiri – Itàla

Location: Itàla, 20km south of Messina.
Starting point: large car park in Itàla below the church, 180m. From Itàla Marina drive along the mountain road to Itàla.
Walking times: Itàla – Sorgente Seddiri 2½ hrs., Sorgente Seddiri – M. Scuderi 1 hr., M. Scuderi – Sorgente Seddiri ¾ hr., Sorgente Seddiri – Itàla 2 hrs.; total time 6¼ hrs.
Ascent: 1200m.
Grade: good standard of fitness required due to length and variation in height. Descent sometimes without paths. Sure-footedness essential. Marked red and white throughout.
Food and accommodation: bar in Itàla.

Bars and restaurants in Itàla Marina.

On the summit of Monte Scuderi there once existed a Byzantine settlement which was destroyed by the Saracens. In the 11th century King Roger I won his first battle against the Saracens in these vast mountains. Out of gratitude he built the Norman basilica SS. Pietro e Paolo in the Croce area of Itàla which is worth a visit.

From the car park in **Itàla** follow the signs for Mannello. Take the turn-off right along the river. On the following right hand bend leave the road to the left (first waymarker at the **Fiume di Mùcari**). 5 mins. later go left over the stream and ascend the narrow path. At the fork keep left and go uphill beside a wall over terraces and steps. Keep right at the fork past an iron gate and cross over a road. The path continues uphill opposite. After 1 hr., shortly after a spring, cross the road again. This path is fairly overgrown as it goes past electricity masts. Back on the road go up round two bends. On the second bend go right and steeply up beside the fence. Having reached an unsurfaced road go right (on the left you can see Monte Scuderi). Keep right at a turn-off (on the left a forest hut). The marked path leads right here along the ridge and keeps crossing over the road. Eventually you walk on the level along the road as far as a col (on the right before that is the return path No. 102/103). At **Portella Salice** (1005m) you can see the Tyrrhenian Sea, Messina and the coast of Calabria.

Go left through the iron gate and after 5 mins. reach the **Sorgente Seddiri** spring. From here the route goes first along a level broad path, then up round a few bends to the summit. The old path begins at the end of the track and meanders to the summit plateau of **Monte Scuderi**. The highest point, which you reach in a few minutes, is visible in the south (be careful of the crevices in the rock!). You can make out Rocca di Novara across Peloritani to the west. Etna can be seen in all its glory in the south and the Cyclopean coast extends to the straits of Messina.

For the descent return the same way as far as the spring and the iron gate. Then go back along the road as far as the afore-mentioned turn-off No. 102/103. Ascend here without paths to a col taking special notice of the waymarkers. Keeping at the same height, cross the left-hand slope. Climb over a ladder to the right, continue along the fence, past other ladders. After a ½ hr. descent climb over a marked ladder to the other side. Walk a short way beside the fence first and then you will see the waymarkers below on a flat head of rock (the Fiume di Mùcari valley on the right, with the ascent route above). Keep on this pathless ridge from now on and climb once more over a marked ladder. The ground is steep and the old mule path is unfortunately not maintained. Cross over a dirt road and continue descending to the Mannello district. Walk through the narrow streets to reach the starting point in **Itàla**.

On the descent to Itàla the path becomes more obvious from Pizzo Scàpola onwards.

6 Dinnamare: Sentiero Girasi

A nature trail with a five-star view

Dinnamare – Puntale Bandiera – Rifo. Girasi – Portella del Vento – Dinnamare

Locations: Messina, Villafranca Tirrena.
Starting point: below Santuario Dinnamare, 1000m. Access from Villafranca Tirrena on the SS 113 towards Messina. Right at the Portella S. Rizzo and 9km as far as the first aerial, then left. The hiking path goes straight ahead leaving the road on a right hand bend. Park on the right.
Walking times: Dinnamare – Casetta Forestale ¾ hr., Casetta Forestale – Rifo. Girasi 1½ hrs., Rifo. Girasi – Portella del Vento 1 hr., Port. del Vento – C. Forestale ½ hr., C. Forestale – car park ¾ hr.; total time 4½ hrs.
Ascent: 400m.
Grade: easy walk. Stopping points with information boards showing the route. A short rocky section on the ascent requires sure-footedness.
Food and accommodation: hotels, restaurants, bars in Messina and Villafranca T., *Agriturismo* in Villaggio Salice near Messina.

The 'antenna sul mare' is the viewing platform of Messina. The start of the walk is at the same time the highest point of the whole route. From here you can enjoy a unique panorama of Messina with the harbour which the Greeks called 'Zankle' (sickle).
The path runs for about ¾ hr. from the **car park** as far as the **Casetta Forestale** with a marvellous view of the straits. A few paces after the little forest house, below P. Bandiera, it descends along a broad path to the right. In the distance you can see Capo Milazzo and the Aeolian islands and the mountain village of Rometta on a rise. Sant. Dinnamare lies above on the right and Pizzo Corvo ahead, which you will walk round later on. Go past the start of the return path, round a bend to the left, through a wooden gate and you come to the red and white waymarkers of the 'Sentiero Italia'. Now follow the signs for the 'Sentiero Girasi'. After ¼ hr. you reach a spring. First of all the path crosses the slope, then you meet the road again. Turn right and

5 mins. later turn off to the right again. Go downhill and after 10 mins. you come to the 'Galleria del Soldato', and shortly afterwards some small stone huts. The path slopes down again past some black pines. Once more on the road, go right and stay on it for about ½ hr. Then, after information board No. 17, turn right into the forest and down to a cross path. Left goes to the **Rifugio Girasi**, a cosy resting place with a spring, but your path goes up to the right. After some wooden railings and past a spring, cross the slope, taking care over a stony section. 20 mins. after that the mountain path widens out into a track. After another ½ hr. you reach the forest hut at **Portella del Vento** where the nature trail starts.

But before the hut and a second circular path, 'Sentiero Brignoli', turn sharp right and go for ½ hr. uphill as far as a col. At this point go downhill first, then after ¼ hr. uphill again, go round a fenced-off chestnut wood to the left. After another 10 mins. you reach the path you came on. Go left up to the military road and turn left again to return in ¾ hr. to the **car park**.

The ferries commute between Messina and Villa San Giovanni, Calabria.

7   Monte Poverello, 1279m

From summit to summit through a remote part of Sicily

Piano Lipantana – Monte Rossimanno – Monte Poverello – Rocca Stefana – Piano Lipantana

Location: San Pier Niceto.
Starting point: Piano Lipantana, 740m. Messina – Palermo motorway, exit Milazzo and drive along the SS 113 for 5km towards Messina as far as the first turn-off S. Pier Niceto (8km). Go steeply up through the village to the cemetery and for 1km to the turn-off right to Lipantana. After 10km, at the end of the tarmac road, park near the villas.
Walking times: Piano Lipantana – M. Rossimanno 1¼ hrs., M. Rossimanno – M. Poverello ¾ hr., M. Poverello – Rocca Stefana 1 hr., Rocca Stefana – spring ¾ hr., spring – car park ½ hr.; total time 4¼ hrs.
Ascent: 670m.
Grade: good sense of direction needed. The walk is not marked and sometimes without paths.
A short section on the descent on Monte Giufa requires sure-footedness.

Food and accommodation: *agriturismo*, bars, *trattorías* in S. Pier Niceto, also hotels in and around Milazzo.

Sicilians celebrate all the festivals as they occur. They are numerous, but the Easter celebrations are the best. In S. Pier Niceto a procession takes place in Holy Week in which a crowd of children, dressed as angels, carry the crucifix. They go from house to house and collect money. In the month of August a festival of local cakes and pastries is held, Sacra del Biscotto. In **Piano Lipantana** go in the direction of the traffic past a green iron gate. The ascent begins left along a track. At a fenced water container leave the track and go left up a steep path which crosses over the little road a few times. The obvious path going along a gentle ridge soon turns into several well-trodden paths. Back on the obvious path you go left (eastwards). Below you are the villas. After a 1 hr. ascent, above a craggy valley, you cross a green plateau. Beyond it the path leads to a boundary fence with a wooden ladder. Over the fence go right, past Rocca Padiglione, to **Monte Rossimanno**. First along the fence, then, straight on across the hollow, you head for the ridge opposite and continue along parallel to it. You can see Monte Poverello. First cross the slope on the right, then head for the **Ula**

Salagone col. From there descend left, past some solitary mountain acorn trees and a spring (bath tub). Leave the broad path and go up the slope on the right. You reach **Monte Poverello** on the mountain ridge. The splendid view takes in the Cyclopean coast with M. Scuderi in the east and Calabria in the north.

Go back down the same path, and climb up again to **Ula Salagone**. Be careful: from the lowest part of the col you descend a few paces straight on in a south-westerly direction to find a hidden, but obvious path. From the small valley take this path left across the slope which has a gently sloping ridge. From here you can see the rocky slopes of Rocca Stefana. Ascend on the left of a series of gentle rises, then on the left of a fence to reach the summit slope and continue up left to **Rocca Stefana** (be careful!). Return to the fence and continue on the left parallel to it (be careful, a rocky steep section, you might possibly need to go round to the right!). Past M. Giufa you reach a notch with a wooden gate. Go downhill on the right. 5 mins. later at a turn-off, wind downhill to the left. Look down on the right into the wild Fiume Toro valley where you can see the road leading out of the valley. Reach the road at a spring through a gate and 20 mins. along this you come through another gate to the starting point in **Piano Lipantana**.

Ascent route to M. Poverello (on the right). M. Scuderi in the background.

8   Punta di Castelluzzo, 1162m

God's very own balcony with a view of Mount Etna

Malvagna – Punta di Castelluzzo – Roccella Valdémone

Locations: Malvagna and Roccella Valdémone, near Francavilla di Sicilia.
Starting point: Piazza Roma in Malvagna, 700m. From the coast along the SS 185 via Francavilla and Móio Alcántara up to Malvagna to the first village square.
Destination: Roccella Valdemona, 650m. From Roccella every morning and evening there's a bus to Móio. Another 3½km to Malvagna, 1 hr.

Walking times: Malvagna – Punta Castelluzzo 1¾ hrs., Punta Castelluzzo – Roccella Valdémone 1½ hrs.; total time 3¼ hrs.
Ascent: 512m, 562m in descent.
Grade: not difficult, but there's a steep section. Obvious, but unmarked paths.
Food and accommodation: bars in Malvagna and Roccella, hotels and *trattorías* in Móio and Francavilla.

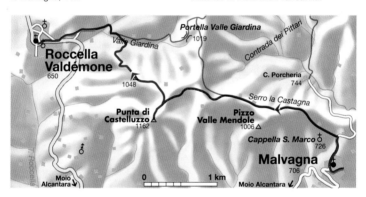

Punta di Castelluzzo reaches its highest point above the Alcántara valley. Two small villages, Malvagna and Roccella Valdémone, stand in picturesque locations, on either side of this mountain range. The view of Mount Etna could not be finer.

From the Piazza in **Malvagna** go through the archway and left beside the cemetery as far as the right hand bend (5 mins.). Here you leave the tarmac road to the left on an ascending path along a fence. After 15 mins. you reach a rib of rock, climb up to the right of it for a short way and find a path along which you cross over the slope on the left. You ascend diagonally over terraces to a col with some solitary oak trees. Now go left fairly steeply up to the ridge where the view opens up of the volcanic cone of Monte Móio, called 'Conca Munti' by the locals. Created by a prehistoric eruption it has inundated the Alcántara valley with masses of lava and mud. In fact grass

Malvagna: a viewing balcony from which to see Etna.

has grown over this catastrophe since then and a little wood has evolved in the crater. Now carry on past the steep slopes of **Pizzo Valle Mendole** up and down along the partly rocky ridge. The path eventually becomes broader and you reach a gate on a flat area. (The road right leads to Roccella V.) Continue parallel to the fence and left up alongside it and again on a ridge over some rocky steps. Roccella V. lies on the right in the valley. Just before the highest point, at some solitary trees, go through an opening in the fence and continue left as far as **Punta di Castelluzzo**. The smoking Etna sits majestically enthroned above the valley. The Naxos coast is visible in the east. In the north you can see the lush forest of Malabotta, through which pilgrims from the surrounding area process in September to the Madonna of Tindari.

For the descent to Roccella go back to the opening in the fence. You will see a track which leads to some chestnut trees. The path swings to the left behind them and descends through the forest.

Sometimes the slope is reinforced with layers of stones. Then it gets a little steeper as the path descends and keeps to the right. After a 15 min. descent go across a broad path. Go right at the next two turn-offs and eventually you reach the tarmac road to walk 1km, past the cemetery, to **Roccella Valdémone**.

9 Rocca di Novara, 1340m

The waymarker of the north-east

Bivio Fondachelli – col – Rocca di Novara

Location: Novara di Sicilia.
Starting point: Bivio Fondachelli, 974m.
On leaving Novara drive south towards
Portella Mandrazzi and for 7km as far as
the turn-off to Fondachelli, park on the left.
Walking times: car park – col ¾ hr., col –
Rocca di Novara ¾ hr., return 1 hr.; total
time 2½ hrs.
Ascent: 370m.
Grade: short walk on obvious paths. The
steep summit slope demands sure-foot-
edness as the path goes over loose
stones in places.
Food and accommodation: bars,
restaurant, rooms for rent in Novara.
Alternative: it's worthwhile making a detour along the ridge of M. Ritagli di Lecca.
On the col before the left turn-off to the
summit, take the broad path to the right for
a short way, go through two gates on the
left and continue along a forest path.
Climb up on the right under the electricity
pylon.
Go anti-clockwise along the edge of the

high plateau, past a precipice at Fantina
valley. The erosion has created bizarre
rock formations.
Descend along the edge through the
forest to the broad path and return the
same way.

The slender Rocca di Novara is particularly striking whether seen from the
3300m high Etna or from the coast. It stands on the edge of the Peloritani
like a waymarker and can be seen clearly from distant areas of the Sicilian
mountains. Its isolated location makes it easy to imagine the kind of panorama it has to offer from its summit.
A few paces along the tarmac road from **Bivio Fondachelli** towards Novara
take the broad forest path which runs parallel to it northwards. Past some
turn-offs and a fire-watch tower you come out of the forest. The path gets
narrower and leads out across an eroded slope. An enormous riverbed has
formed in the broad Fantina valley. Once you've arrived at the **col** you can
see the pine forest on M. Ritagli di Lecca (see alternative). Go up left at the
fork and towards Rocca di Novara. You come to a hilltop and from here you
can make out the town of Novara. Beyond, on the coast, is the pilgrim
church of Tindari high above the cliffs. Turn to the left and shortly afterwards
take the path uphill to the right. Then you come to a gap in the rocks on a
high flat area. The steep ascent up to the summit begins here.

Keeping to the main path you can zigzag uphill without any scrambling. Having reached the top, the summit of **Rocca di Novara** appears unexpectedly with a broad hilltop where you can take your time and enjoy the splendid panorama. All the Peloritani can be seen in the east as far as Calabria, the Aeolian islands in the north and even the Madonie in the west. The soft contours of Nebrodi begin to emerge and in the south, Mount Etna.

You go carefully back down the summit slope and return along the same path to the **Bivio Fondachelli**.

On the ascent you can see Novara and the Santuario di Tindari by the sea.

10 Tholos of Ponticelli, 1350m

Archaeology under the Nebrodi sun

Rifugio Montano – Piano di Nocera – Contrada Ponticelli – Portella Cùfali – Rifugio Montano

Locations: Raccuia and Floresta.
Starting point: Buculica, Rifo. Montano, 1013m. At the northern end of Floresta drive towards Polverello and take the first left-hand turn-off (at present sign-posted). Opposite the turn-off, a narrow tarmac side road goes down from a hill-top straight on, 3.5km to Raccuia. Drive past the houses of Passofavazzo as far as Buculica. Just before the new Rifo. Montano (left) you reach a water trough (right). Park here.
Walking times: Rifo. Montano – Piano di Nocera 1 hr., Piano di Nocera – Ponticelli ½ hr., Ponticelli – Portella Cùfali ½ hr., Portella Cùfali – Rifo. Montano ½ hr.; total time 2½ hrs.

Ascent: 340m.
Grade: unmarked route with a short section without paths on the ascent, otherwise on obvious paths.
Food and accommodation: bars, restaurants in Floresta, *agriturismo* in Raccuia.
NB: from Buculica in the direction of the traffic northwards, keeping right at turn-offs, you reach a junction 'Case Pirato'. Numerous *tholos* lie scattered over the pastures in this hamlet. From here it is possible to drive along the road left, via Fondachello to Raccuia and continue via Ucria, Castelumberto and Naso to the coast and thereby get to know a little bit of Sicily's unexpected interior.

In the mountains of Nebrodi, between Raccuia, Floresta and Montalbano, there are round stone constructions strewn across pastures and in the forests. The little domed buildings, called *tholos* or *cubburo*, have a diameter of 345cm at the most, of which the wall is already 100cm thick. This ingenious construction has a 'dome' with a smoke hole cover on top and has a perfect stability and doesn't let in any water. The building material is crystalline sandstone from the area. Dry stone walls, ie. without mortar, have

1. *The supporting sub-structure.*
2. *Diagram of the 'dome'.*
3. *The 'dome'.*

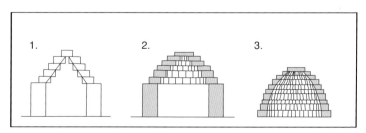

been erected around the constructions which have not been renovated. Giovanni Barone, a young architect from Raccuia, examined over 100 of these constructions during his studies, across an area of 90 sq. km., and established that their locations were mainly at an altitude of 840 to 1370m. Because of their round shape and conical roof it is suspected that they date from prehistoric times and were constantly rebuilt or restored over the centuries. Since they were used by the shepherds then (as they are today) for shelter, the conclusion is that they lay on an important and regular shepherds' path. Comparisons have been made with constructions from the legendary Troja (burial chambers) up to the Trulli of Apulien (dwellings).

Go from the car park back along the road and past the **Rifo. Montano**. Behind the next group of houses go immediately left up along a path which has been paved at the start. On the left, below the steep slopes of M. Cùfali, lie the derelict houses of **Buculica**. The path goes uphill between the high gorse, becomes stony and brings you across the **Giangali stream**. You walk parallel to it at the edge of some pasture-land and past a water container where the path becomes a green ramp. The road runs above which you will use for the return. Go through an opening in the fence on the right, over the stream again and come to a water trough and a *tholos*. There you discover some restored *tholos* as well which have been turned into huts.

Ponticelli I. Giovanni Barone has examined over 100 of these curious constructions.

47

Continue left parallel to a fence above the little valley. At the next fenced water container the path gets lost on the eroded slope. To the right above you can see some derelict foundations. Continue ascending without paths as you go past them, then keep to the right and go round the slope. On the right, at the edge of a clearing, go as far as a cross fence by the forest. Slip through a gap in the fence and then turn sharp right under large pine trees along a broad path which leads up to the left. In the middle of a wood of oak, pine, beech and chestnut trees you come across another *tholos* where at present the smoke hole cover is missing. Water has seeped in causing vegetation to grow inside which could soon dislodge the stones that are covered in moss. 5 mins. later, at a cross path, go left and then straight ahead past a right-hand turn-off. When you come out of the forest you reach the road between Floresta (right) and Portella Cùfali (left). Cross over at the left-hand bend and ascend a firebreak up to the pine wood opposite. Without turning off carry on over partly rocky ground and keep going straight on south-eastwards with Etna visible on the horizon. The forest path goes round a long S-bend at the edge of the wood to the **Contrada Ponticelli**, a plateau where there's a large restored *tholos*, the so-called Ponticelli I. From the edge of the plain you can see San Piero Pati in the Timeto valley,

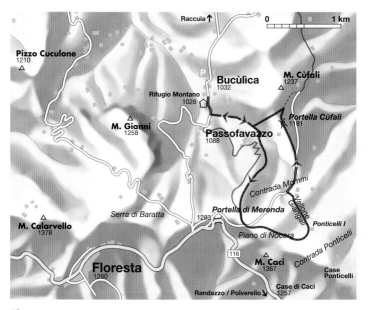

Orange groves on the slopes of Nebrodi.

with Capo di Milazzo behind and the Aeolian islands close-by. In the east between Montalbano and the majestic Rocca di Novara you catch sight of the Argimusco rocks (Walk 11). Walk left along the fence and come to some more well-preserved buildings. At a little wall descend a short way along an old trading path.

The path swings down to the right above a valley. From here you can see the road which divides a conspicuous rib of rock. Go left above a hut to the road and to the right along this to the rib of rock where you will see on the left the valley which you came up. Shortly after the rib of rock leave the road to the left. Remains of the old trading path lead up towards M. Cùfali where there's a shepherds' hut on the slope. Just in front, in the **Portella Cùfali**, you can see the remains of a property on the left between enormous holly trees. Numerous derelict *tholos* are to be found nearby and below them, a circular pond.

Descend left along well-trodden paths, past the pond, to arrive at the green ramp again and go through the opening in the fence back along the path you came on to the **Rifugio Montana**.

11 The Argimusco rocks

The megaliths of Sicily

Fontana Scavi – Portella Calvagna – 'Dea Neolitica' – Fontana Scavi

Location: Montalbano Elicona.
Starting point: Fontana Scavi, 1200m. From Montalbano towards Malabotta there are signs pointing to the 'Rocce dell'Argimusco' leading up out of the village. At the turn-off (sign-posted left to Tripi) drive right along the SP 115 towards Floresta. (The direct, sign-posted stretch of road to Floresta does not go to the SS

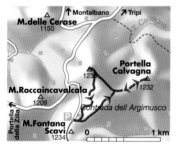

115!). From here go 1.2km to a small tarmac road and along this for another 0.5km past a wooden gate. Immediately afterwards there's a parking bay on the left.
Walking times: Fontana Scavi – Portella Calvagna ½ hr., P. Calvagna – second viewpoint ½ hr., second viewpoint – Fontana Scavi ½ hr.; total time 1½ hrs.
Ascent: 50m.
Grade: the route goes across open ground on unsurfaced roads, meadows and beaten tracks.
Food and accommodation: bars, restaurants, guest house in Montalbano.
NB: on the SP 115 towards Floresta you can drive another 3km to Portella della Zilla where the 'Ovile del Gesuito' can be found on the left of the road, an old shepherd's house with a sheep pen in the rock. After 1km on the right there are other interesting 'monuments' to see.

Gaetano Pantano, Professor for Art History from Montalbano, dealt with the existence of a megalithic people in Sicily in a volume of pictures with the title 'Megaliti di Sicilia'. His theory relates the plateau of Argimusco to a place of cult worship and he sees the monolithic rocks as shaped by human hand, even as symbols erected for cult worship. Near the sandstone rocks of Argimusco there are deposits which evolved through the overlaying of other layers and the resulting warmth of pressure just like baking. When the softer surface was taken away they remained behind as a compact component of the sedimentary mass. Variations in temperature, rain and wind have acted as 'sculptors'.

From the car park at **Fontana Scavi** go through the wooden gate onto the high plateau of Argimusco along a dirt road. The first rocks on the left are known as female and male fertile symbols. At the first turn-off carry on right along the track across soft meadows. The path turns into a track again which curves round to the right across the plateau to the elevation, **Portella Calvagna**, 1232m, to which you ascend. From the top you can enjoy a beautiful panorama and you look down on Tripi below in the valley. Rocca di

Novara rises in the east which looks itself like a monolith. Go back to the bend in the track. A little path bears right. Walk along this towards the **second viewpoint** where there's a conspicuous box-shaped rock. Cross the plain and you reach the highest point of the walk. In the rock there's a tub-shaped depression hewn by human hand. Today, shepherds still make these kind of rock depressions to be used as water troughs for the animals. Montalbano with its huge castle is in sight, but also the church at Capo Tindari and the Aeolian islands. From here you have a good view across the rock towers with their bizarre shapes.

Go back downhill, but walk diagonally to the first towers on the right. Go around their weather-beaten flank on the right and you will see the next group of rocks. This is the best point from where to see the **'Dea Neolitica'**. Take a closer look at them and then on the way back to the starting point at **Fontana Scavi**, zigzag between the rock formations to appreciate their fantastic shapes.

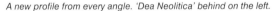

A new profile from every angle. 'Dea Neolitica' behind on the left.

12 Madonna of Tindari, 279m

Lakes, Black Madonna and Roman basilica

Oliveri – lakes – pilgrim church – Oliveri

Location: Oliveri.

Starting point: Oliveri beach. Along the Palermo – Messina motorway, take the Falcone exit, go left to Oliveri. In the middle of the town follow 'Laghetti di Marinello' signs at the roundabout for just under 1km as far as the starting point, park just before the start of a road with a green line down the middle.

Walking times: Oliveri – Capo Tindari ¾ hr., C. Tindari – pilgrim church ¾ hr., pilgrim church – Oliveri ¾ hr.; total time 2¼ hrs.

Ascent: 300m.

Grade: this walk is easy, it only requires sure-footedness on the ascent to the col at C. Tindari. Obvious paths, but not marked.

Food and accommodation: numerous possibilities in Oliveri, Marinello and Falcone.

NB: just before reaching the pilgrim church, the path goes through private property. If you ask for permisson you can walk across the restaurant terrace.

The festival of the Black Madonna at Tindari has been celebrated on the 8th September for over 400 years. The importance of this strategically well-placed town goes back to classical antiquity. The lagoons have recently been placed under environmental protection: Riserva Naturale Laghetti di Marinello.

Begin the walk on **Oliveri** beach to the left. Past the last house you reach a broad path. After walking for ½ hr. go right at the fork in the path. You walk between two **lakes** towards the promontory, **Capo Tindari**. Just before, on the verdant slope, a zigzag path leads up to a col at the Capo Tindari. From the col go along beside the green bushes, gain height on an obvious path and eventually reach a mountain ridge (below there's a farm). Climb up to the right on this ridge and arrive at a plateau. Keeping to the right across a road you go left through a gate and then come to a fork. Go left here and continue along beside the archaeological excavations of ancient Tindari towards the Madonna sanctuary. Through an iron gate on the left you come to the terrace of a restaurant and up the steps to the large Piazza in front of the **pilgrim church**. From the forecourt head towards the church's fassade, keep on the right and descend some steps at the end of a side road. From here you can see the Peloritani mountain range with Rocca di Novara.

Descend along a fence and head for the plateau you can see below. Go left there at the fork and stay on the broad path leading downhill. Afterwards you come through two pasture fences and continue across a hollow with a little stream. From here you descend a broad path, under which there's a water channel, to a lemon grove with an iron gate. The path leads left to a junction. Go right here, left at the following cross path and under the car and railway bridge you come to an unsurfaced road. Go left and round a bend to the right where you meet the path along the beach you came on from **Oliveri**. Right goes to the parking area.

Santuario di Tíndari stands high above the coast. The Peloritani in the background.

13 Rocche del Crasto, 1315m

From rocks that can speak

Longi – Filippelli – Rocca che Parla – Rocche del Crasto – Longi

Location: Longi.

Starting point: war memorial in Longi, 623m. Between Capo d'Orlando and S. Ágata di Militello the SP 157 turns off at Capri Leone and goes via Mirto and Frazzanó to Longi. Go through Longi past the church. Parking almost at the end of the village at a memorial near a petrol station.

Walking times: Longi – Filippelli ½ hr., Filippelli – Rocche del Crasto 1½ hrs., Rocche del Crasto – Fontana del Bosco 1 hr., Fontana del Bosco – Longi ¾ hr.; total time 3¾ hrs.

Ascent: 800m.

Grade: the paths are not marked, but they are for the most part obvious and easy to negotiate. The second part of the descent requires a good sense of direction.

Food and accommodation: bars, restaurants and *agriturismo* in Longi and Galati Mamertino.

NB: it's best to leave Longi via Portella Gazzana through the wild Rosmarino

valley, with stops in Alcara li Fusi and Militello Rosmarino.

Krastos was the first town which Aeneas' companions built after the flight from Troy. Rocche del Crasto, as its name implies, is supposed to have been the 'location'. Longi dates back to Castrum Longum. The myth took shape when the Normans in the 12th century extended the ancient fortification which can still be visited today.

A cobbled road begins opposite the war memorial in **Longi** (later Via Sta. Croce). Using the steps past a few wayside shrines you come to a road which leads left to the cemetery. Go right, over a bridge, then immediately left, up the steps of the old trading path. Above the Campo Sportivo zigzags take you to the upper part of the little valley which you crossed over on the bridge. You come to a turn-off here (left is the return path). Continue right and arrive at the hamlet of **Filippelli**. Pizzo Stifani rises up behind. Along a row of houses you reach a viewing terrace. Galati Mamertino, San Salvatore and other places cling to the steep slopes or sit enthroned on the mountain peaks above the deeply-cut Valle del Fitalia. The Aeolian islands emerge from the sea. Longi lies below with the pink-washed central church of San

Michele. Left of the terrace there's a wayside shrine for the patron saint, S. Leone. The path climbs straight up the mountain slope opposite. You gradually approach the smoothly polished, ivy covered rock face of **Rocca che Parla**. There was supposed to be an echo here at one time. The rock has remained silent since avaricious people dug for legendary treasure on the mountain. The path joins a broad track. Go right below the rock face, past a derelict hut, to a col. You come through an opening in the fence to a broad cross path and see the village of Mistretta on a ridge with Madonie

Villages sit enthroned on the rises of Nebrodi.

behind. Descend left. The 'talking rock' towers up left with several rises and you can see Rocche del Crasto ahead.

Then you come to the **Sette Fontane** spring. Go left along the track lying above and to the next col. The highest peaks of Nebrodi can be seen ahead, across extensive areas of pasture. Leave the track here to the right and go along a well-trodden path at the edge of a field, beside a pasture fence, up to the conspicuous gap in the rocks where, keeping left along an obvious path, you reach **Rocche del Crasto**. The landscape does not want for beauty and contrasts. It stretches from the Tyrrhenian Sea across fertile orchards and limestone mountains which then turn abruptly into gentle pastures, enclosed by the largest expanses of forest in Sicily.

Go back to the track along the same path, downhill and past three turnings off to the left. They all lead up into the forest. Immediately after the third there's a multiple junction where the paths bear left and right from the track. Follow the narrow steeply sloping path on the left into the wood which levels out further down. Past a broad path to the left you keep going downhill to the point where the path divides. The path goes right to the tarmac road, but you go up left and straight on past a left hand turn-off. 5 mins. later, just before the Fontana del Bosco spring (drinking water), take a left-hand turn-off uphill and leave the forest through a barrier. At a right hand turn-off which leads to a farm house, go straight on to a left-hand bend where the path goes up into the wood. Just on the bend turn off right and go across a level clearing to an edge. From here you can see Filippelli and the road with the cemetery.

Way below lies a small stone house which your route will take you past. Descend through some openings in the fence, one shortly followed by another, and through a last one on the left you start the traverse of the slope. The path leads partly through undergrowth and gradually descends.

Before the wood cross over a little stream, keep right at the fork and left past the stone house, through a barrier into the wood. Once out in the open again, the path goes across the slope on the left and after crossing a stream you come to the turn-off where you made your ascent. Go right and down to **Longi** along the path you came on.

Longi, at the foot of Rocca che Parla, the 'talking rock'.

14 Monte Pelato, 1567m

The barren mountain in the forests of Nebrodi

Sorgiva Nocita – Caserma Mafauda – Monte Pelato – Portella Calcare – Caserma Mafauda – Sorgiva Nocita

Locations: Caronìa and Capizzi.
Starting point: Sorgiva Nocita, 1429m. From Nicosia via Capizzi or from Caronìa via Portella dell'Òbolo you take the provincial road SP 168 into the Nebrodi forests. From the Òbolo pass, after 1½km in the direction of Capizzi a tarmac road descends left. At present, the tarmac ends after 4km, but the road continues for 1km over gravel to Sorgiva Nocita (picnic area).

Walking times: Sorgiva Nocita – Caserma Mafauda ½ hr., Mafauda – M. Pelato 1 hr., M. Pelato – Mafauda 1 hr., Mafauda – Sorgiva Nocita ½ hr.; total time 3 hrs.
Ascent: 320m.
Grade: gentle walk on clear, unmarked paths.
Food and accommodation: a good selection in Caronìa and on the coast. See also Walk 15.

Monte Pelato, also called Pizzo Pilato, lies in the heart of the Nebrodi nature reserve which is covered in forest and abounding in water. Nevertheless its summit allows a panorama of the seemingly endless woodland and a lot more besides. The small village of Capizzi nestles into the mountain slopes. Its inhabitants have made a living from breeding cattle for generations and they produce excellent milk products, like ricotta and other cheese. You shouldn't miss the slightly sour variety, Próvola, exclusive to Capizzi.

Begin the walk at **Sorgiva Nocita** along the road in the direction of the traffic and come to **Caserma Mafauda**. Just before the little houses follow a path bearing left into the forest. Behind a water trough walk along the broad path northwards and leisurely uphill. Go past a left hand turn-off with a gate. Marvellous examples of beech trees, some solitary pendunculate oaks, dominate the forest up to the summit region. Hollies thrive in the undergrowth and also Daphne, the yellowish green spring flowering plant in the south. At the next turn-off you come to **Portella Donna Vile**. The main path leads downhill through a gate. Go right and now up parallel to a boundary fence, staying on the ridge. Keeping to the right at a rib of rock, look for a way across.

Afterwards you come to a clearing and curve round to the right along the boundary fence eastwards up to **Monte Pelato**, 1567m. From the top you can see the Aeolian islands in the north and in front, the village of S. Fratello sits boldly on a peak. The softly undulating landscape is only relieved by M. Soro with the aerials and the deep S. Fratello valley. Here, in autumn, there's a whole range of shimmering colours from bright yellow to dark brown. In the west you can see Monte Castelli and Sambughetti on the Colle Contrasto above Capizzi and below you, the Mafauda forestry house.

Leave the summit to the south and descend along the ridge into the wood. The forest path joins a forest road at **Portella Calcare**.

Go right here. Straight past a turn-off the path winds its way down to a tarmac road. Go right and carry on to the unsurfaced road to the **Caserma Mafauda**. Straight on from here you reach **Sorgiva Nocita** along the path you came on.

In autumn the forests of Nebrodi explode into colour.

15 Monte Sambughetti, 1558m

The granaries of Rome between Etna and Enna

Forest entrance – Monte Trippaturi – Monte Sambughetti – forest entrance

Locations: Mistretta and Nicosia.
Starting point: forest entrance on M. Sambughetti, 1100m. From the SS 117 Mistretta – Nicosia a forest road bears right just under 1km after the Colle del Contrasto, just before the 29km marker stone. Park before the barrier.
Walking times: forest entrance – M. Trippaturi 1¾ hrs., M. Trippaturi – M. Sambughetti ¾ hr., M. Sambughetti – resting place ½ hr., resting place – forest entrance 1 hr.; total time 4 hrs.
Ascent: 500m.
Grade: easy walk exclusively on forest roads.
Food and accommodation: from the starting point 11km towards Nicosia Motel. Simple hotel in Capizzi.

The mountain area of Sicily's interior, the southern Monti Nebrodi, is a softly undulating high mountain range. The extensive agricultural land and the wooded mountain slopes between Etna and Enna were already an attraction in classical antiquity and were used intensively as Rome's granaries. The rock dwellings and the forest of Sperlinga as well as the villages of Nicosia and Capizzi, hardly visited by tourists, still retain an air of 'typical Sicilian'.

After a short walk from the barrier at the **forest entrance** you come to a turn-off. Go left through the wooden gate and continue along the forest road. You can see the rocky slope of M. Campanito opposite, and Etna on the left. Through pasture fences you come to a turn-off (information board with plan of the area), go right along the equally broad path and clamber over other barriers. After walking for 1 hr., at a viewpoint at 1360m, the path swings to the left. Further on you come past a left-hand turn-off with a gate: the return path. Continue at the same height right around the northern slopes of M. Sambughetti. On the right you can see the foothills of M. Trippaturi. A wide valley runs below and the Bosco della Giumenta. The path is lined with holly trees, poplars, oaks and beech, waymarked in orange in places and eroded. Now and then it descends for a short way. On the continuing ascent, on a hill-top, you go left into the forest and along the fence where you meet a broad path. Go uphill round a few bends and through a barrier to a junction. Go left here and in ¼ hr. you reach the summit of **Monte Sambughetti** with a red and white checked trig point. Now the marvellous panorama is complete: the Aeolian islands in the north, Madonie enthroned in the west, and Bosco di Sperlinga lying in the south. Nicosia and Cerami are visible as well as the small village of Capizzi on the left at the foot of M. Pelato.

The descent goes back along the same path as far as the fork. Then keep to the left going downhill. At the following fork ascend left (the main path goes down right to Poiada). You reach the col between M. Sambughetti and M. Campanito. Go through a gate left to the 'Mulattiera di Nevaruoe' and begin the descent which leads through a bizarre rocky landscape interspersed with numerous types of holly. After a ¼ hr. descent you reach a quiet **resting place** on the right of the path. There are stone tables and benches in front of a cave in the rock. Past this you come to a gate and meet the ascent path. Go right and return in 1 hr. to the **forest entrance** along the path you came on.

Cerami and Troina in front of Etna.

16 Pizzo Catarineci, 1660m

On the edge of Madonie

Geraci – Pietra Giordano – col – Cozzo di Raimondo – Pizzo Catarineci

Location: Geraci Sículo.
Starting point: from the well at the end of Geraci, 1011m. At the southern edge of Geraci, on the SS 286, there's a large stone well on the right, a bar and in between a tarmac road. It's recommended that you park around here.
Walking times: Geraci – Pietra Giordano 1½ hrs., P. Giordano – col ¼ hr., col – Pizzo Catarineci ¾ hr., return 2 hrs.; total time 4½ hrs.
Ascent: 700m.
Grade: easy walk. Marked as far as the col (wooden board, No. 10). Afterwards without paths, but the terrain does not present any problems in clear weather.

Food and accommodation: hotels, bars, restaurants in Geraci, Gangi and Petralia Sottana.
See also Walk 17.

At the edge of the 'Parco delle Madonie' with the shapes of its characteristic limestone landscape a row of sandstone peaks rise up high. Pizzo Catarineci is one of these, which has an abundance of water. Bottles are filled with the precious fluid in Geracis mineral water factory and exported.

Walk from the well in **Geraci** along the tarmac road for about 10 mins., past a hotel and a little transformer house, as far as a gravel track. Leave the tarmac here to the left. After 10 mins., on the second bend, bear right from the gravel track. The narrow path continues up and down over some river gullies, and then along a slope between holly trees (*Ilex aquifolium*). It ascends westwards with a view of Geraci Sículo and S. Mauro Castelverde behind. 15 mins. after the turn-off you leave the obvious path to the left and follow the path No. 10 past the foundations of old huts with a round sheep pen. Immediately afterwards keep right and go up the slope. Opposite you see the Catarineci ridge, on the right areas of pasture-land and on the left a light beech wood. The path swings gently to the left and you come to an aqueduct with a row of water containers. Walk along the aqueduct through part of a wood (picnic tables). **Pietra Giordano**, a higher area of huge boulders, is on the right of the path. Here, a unique landscape opens up. A water trough stands on the right on an area of pasture. The path gets narrower and winds its way towards this through bizarre holly trees. Sometimes it gets lost amongst huge boulders. Head for the obvious path opposite which leads up to a **col** (1467m) a bit further on to the right. When you arrive at the top, the highest peaks of Madonie give the scenery its character. Path

No. 10 goes from here down to the Casa Gorgonero and to the tarmac road between Petralie and Piano Battaglia.

Do not take this path, instead go left from the notch, along the rocky knolls. In a conspicuous cleft you change over to the left onto a plateau, **Piano Raimondo**. Here too, you walk parallel to some rocky elevations. The last one in the link is **Cozzo di Raimondo**. You come to a col below it and in the south-east you can see Pizzo Catarineci. Descend left and go uphill between juniper bushes to the next cleft. You recognise Pietra Giordano above the beech wood below. Now stay on the ridge and keeping to the right, ascend across some rocks to a high plateau and from here go left up to the **Pizzo Catarineci**. In the south, quite nearby, lie the two Petralie and in the east below, the marvellous plateau of Piano Catarineci.

Return on the same path to **Geraci**. After you have left the aqueduct behind, you need to pay special attention to the route up to the gravel track to avoid getting lost!

The holly trees at Pietra Giordano.

17 Vallone Canna

Exciting walk through the wild Canna gorge

Casa La Pazza – Vallone Canna – Casa Sambuchi – Casa La Pazza

Locations: Petralia Sottana and Petralia Soprana on the south slopes of the Madonie.

Starting point: provincial road SP 54, above Casa La Pazza, 1410m. From Piano Battaglia, Rifo. Marini head towards Petralie. At the fourth car park, after 3km, park on the left. It's 13km coming from Petralia Sottana.

Walking times: La Pazza – gorge ¾ hr., through the gorge to Casa Sambuchi 1¾ hrs., Casa Sambuchi – La Pazza 1¾ hrs.; total time 4¼ hrs.

Ascent: 500m.

Grade: demanding walk. The gorge is strewn with high boulders and some tricky overgrown areas (don't forget the secateurs). In winter and after melting snow and rain, the conditions are more difficult. The easy return path goes along partly marked paths (little wooden boards).

Food and accommodation: bars and pizzeria in Petralia Soprana, also a hotel in Petralia Sottana. Rifo. Marini (CAI hut) at Piano Battaglia and Ostello di Gioventù at Portella colla. *Agriturismo* Gorgo Nero on the SP 54 towards Petralie.

This energetic and exciting hike goes through a limestone gorge which is one of the few passable gorges of the Madonie and is hardly ever walked. The peaceful return path from farm to farm is quite a contrast. The abandoned Casa La Pazza belongs to a project of the 'Parco delle Madonie', whereby several traditional huts have been restored.

From the car park walk in the direction of the traffic down the tarmac road. After a few minutes you reach the sign-posted turn-off to the Casa La Pazza. You are immersed in a fascinating landscape, craggy and wild – on the right the slopes of M. San Salvatore, with Pizzo di Canna ahead. Go down the broad path (No. 15) and come to the **Casa La Pazza** with a *pagghiaru*, a shelter covered in rushes. 50 paces after that you leave the broad path along a well-trodden path down the slope towards Pizzo Canna and the gorge which is already visible. Much lower down you come to the stream

From Casa La Pazza there's a view of Pizzo Canna (left) and the gorge.

bed of the Canna and walk parallel to it as far as a clearing. On the left of this go to the ruins of a water pump, leave this on the right and begin the descent into the **Vallone Canna**. Take great care from here when it's wet.

After a while the gorge descends and the tall rock faces of Pizzo Canna and steep towers rise up above. From now on you need to scramble, jump and climb hand over hand down over several steep steps. Some are between 4 and 8m high and smoothly polished. Sometimes you can go round the steep steps left or right through dense undergrowth. It can take up to ¾ hr. until you reach the cone of rubble of Pizzo Canna.

Now the steps are shallower and after another ½ hr. the valley flattens out. There are springs on the path and there's water running in the riverbed. At a height of 960m there's a gap in the fence on the left. From here walk along the right hand bank, sometimes above the river, and then go out of the valley changing over a few times from one side to the other. After ¼ hr. before a broad path goes up right (with wooden railings) go across the river to the left and go uphill along a broad path to an opening in the fence in 10 mins. to a farm: **Casa Sambuchi**. Looking back you can see the tall rock towers of the gorge, especially the imposing Pizzo Canna.

Go through the farm (if the shepherds are there it's normal to exchange a few words with them!), keep to the right of the houses and go through fence openings up to a hill with large trees. There's a round sheep pen here with a cattle trough and a track below. Go along this to the right and immediately left at the first turn-off.

The ascent begins along the marked path No. 14 which leads in ½ hr. through a holm oak wood to a gate. First go a short way beyond this along the broad path and then stay to the left of a fence. A well-trodden path brings you to the top. Once on the broad path again go left and come to a hut. Go past it to the right and continue left through the opening in the fence. An obvious path goes to a spring, swings to the left and crosses the top of the slope. You can see Pizzo Canna ahead and a fence above on the right which you ascend towards. At this point, ¾ hr. from Casa Sambuchi, there's a large oak tree beyond which you come to the path No. 15 leading right to Piano Pomo and Castelbuono. Go left and look across the Vallone Sambuchi and Canna over to Etna.

Descend to a water trough and uphill again to a plateau below Pizzo Canna. Keeping right you catch sight of the road in front. Descend along the main path to the **Vallone Faguara** bridge.

After ascending again and keeping left, go along path No. 15 eventually to **Casa La Pazza**. Between Pagghiaru and the shepherds' huts go up to the road and right to the car park.

The end is in sight when you see water in the river bed.

18 Monte San Salvatore, 1912m

Nebrodi firs, Madonna of the Angels and other saints

Forest entrance – Vallone Madonna degli Angeli – Piano Iola – Monte San Salvatore – Madonna dell'Alto – Piano Iola – forest entrance

Location: Polizzi Generosa.
Starting point: entrance gate for the forestry administration, 1240m. From Polizzi Generosa along the SP 119 towards Portella Colla and Piano Battaglia you come to an iron gate after 8.7km. Park here or a few metres further on. Coming from Portella Colla it's 3.3km.
Walking times: forest entrance – Sentiero Natura fork (SN) ½ hr., SN fork – Piano Iola 1¾ hrs., Piano Iola – M. S. Salvatore 1½ hrs., M. S. Salvatore – col 20 mins., detour to Madonna dell'Alto 20 mins., col

– Rifo. Forestale 1 hr., Rifo. Forestale – forest entrance ¾ hr.; total time 6¼ hrs.
Ascent: 900m.
Grade: long, but easy walk on obvious, marked paths (wooden boards). The descent from M. S. Salvatore to the col is without paths, not marked and rather steep.
Food and accommodation: bars, restaurants, rooms for rent in Polizzi G. A hotel in Castellana Sícula. See also Walk 17.

Situated at the southern edge of the Madonie, M. San Salvatore offers magnificent and contrasting views. The path goes through a craggy landscape with bizarre rock formations and endemic firs. This landscape has an air of ancient sacredness about it – perhaps the source of the valley and mountain names.

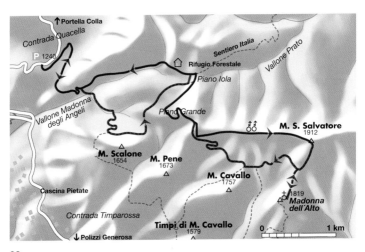

Nebrodi firs, Abies nebrodiensis.

Beyond the iron gate at the **forestry entrance** go along the forest road which leads uphill at the edge of the dramatic rocky landscape of Quacella. After just under ½ hr. you will see Polizzi G. in the south lying in its picturesque location on a mountain ridge and the endless hilly region beyond. Below lies the deeply-cut valley of Madonna degli Angeli. At the turn-off leave the track to the right along the Sentiero Natura, cross over the valley of the Madonna of the Angels and enter a beautiful mixed wood.

The great rarity in this wood is the *Abies nebrodiensis*, which is threatened by extinction and can only be seen here in the Madonie. This endemic

Nebrodi fir was so named because the whole mountain area in North Sicily was once called Nebrodi. It has difficulty in propagating itself and stands under natural protection. One of the protective measures is to sow seeds and cross-breed it with other species, for example the white fir, and also to carefully maintain the slopes on which it grows. You will find a few examples along this nature trail.

Gain height round some zigzags and come past the right hand turn-off to Polizzi. At 1640m the path levels out and leads through a little pine wood and across meadows. Above you on the left you can see some instruments for measuring precipitation. A broad path begins again along here which you ascend to a rounded hill-top.

At the next turn-off continue along the roadway. On the left you can see into the upper valley of the Madonna and on the far side of it, the forestry house. At **Piano Iola** you come to a cross path and you go right (left for the return). With marvellous views to the south and west you come to a fork at a barrier. On the right the path goes to the Madonna dell'Alto chapel and this is the way you return.

Continue beyond the barrier, past a left-hand turn-off and a row of aerials. At the last hill covered with aerials go right. On the ridge you can see the highest point ahead, walk forwards and look for a path just to the left descending through the dwarf beech trees to a col and up to **Monte San Salvatore**. An iron trig post marks the highest point. Look across the broad Imera valley to Mount Etna in the east. The village of Gangi clings to a smaller pyramid-shaped mountain in front. Both of the Petralies are visible and in the north, the Carbonara massif. The shrine of Madonna dell'Alto stands on a secondary summit in the south. Keeping to the right descend the slope in this direction without paths, come through the wood to a broad path and onto the col between the two summits. Here there's a spring with drinking water.

In 10 mins. take the broad path to Mount Calvary with the **Madonna dell'Alto** shrine, a chapel with a pilgrims' house and the venue for religious festivals almost all year round. On the 15th August, when the festival of the Madonna is celebrated, thousands of pilgrims travel up here in jeeps and carts or come on foot from the surrounding areas.

Back on the col go left, keep right at all turn-offs and ascend to the fork with a barrier. The descent begins here. Go back along the path you came on to the point where you joined it at Piano Iola. Then go straight on along a new route, past the **Rifo. Forestale** (spring and picnic area) and past the turn-off of the Sentiero Natura, then back along the path to the starting point, the **forestry entrance**.

You can see Polizzi Generosa and the hills in the south through the Vallone Madonna degli Angeli.

19 Monte dei Cervi, 1794m

The gorge of hell and a pan with a handle

Vivaio Forestale Piano Noce – Vallone Inferno – Monte dei Cervi – La Padella – Vivaio Forestale

Location: Polizzi Generosa.
Starting point: Vivaio Forestale Piano Noce, 1028 m. Drive along the SP 119 from Polizzi Generosa 6km towards Piano Battaglia and Portella Colla as far as the turn-off to Vivaio (tree nursery). From Portella Colla it's 5.6km. Another 500m down to the iron gate.
Walking times: Vivaio – V. Inferno 1 hr., gorge walk 1¼ hrs., V. Inferno – M. Cervi 1 hr., M. Cervi – start of Padella 1 hr., walk

through Padella 1 hr., end of Padella – Vivaio 1 hr.; total time 6¼ hrs.
Ascent: 900m.
Grade: easy-going terrain round M. Cervi becomes demanding and hazardous as you go through the Vallone Inferno and cross the Padella.
Only marked in places (wooden boards, No. 23).
Food and accommodation: see Walks 17 and 18.

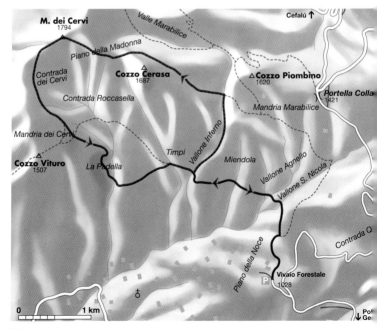

Forest people from Polizzi G. at the start of the Vallone Inferno.

From Polizzi Generosa you can see the M. Cervi massif. The enormous area of subsidence there is fascinating and looks like a pan (Italian *padella*). It was created by colossal movements of the earth's crust. Together with the numerous limestone gorges which cut into the slope, the pan also acquired a handle at a later date, although it is now completely overgrown. You can walk through the Vallone Inferno on the right of the pan.

On the right next to the iron gate from the **Vivaio Forestale Piano Noce** go through the wooden gate and start the marked route No. 23 along a road to the Cozzo Vituro. At a barrier in a hollow ascend right and continue straight on at the next turn-off. This road ascends leisurely across the slopes which are soon covered in forest and the higher you get, the more open the view across the tree nursery to Polizzi Generosa. You come past various valleys and at a cross fence reach the start of the **Vallone Inferno**. Go up here on the right and enter the broad, overgrown valley through a gate. Go directly across the big stones in the middle. Steep rocks line the gorge and in places high up are overgrown with ivy. You can see from the spines strewn about that porcupines live here. There's no water in the gorge, but take care when it's wet!

Clamber up over a few steep steps and you have to work your way through dense vegetation every now and then. After an S-bend the ground begins to level out. Now the path goes across pastures until you're out of the gorge. A landscape of forest and pastures greets us with the Pizzo Antenna massif ahead. Ascend left, mainly between forest and stony ridge.

After ½ hr., at a conspicuous rock along the ridge, you see the wooded M. Cervi in front. The path there is interrupted by a wooded rocky section. Go round this on the right: first a short way down into the forest and across some clearings. Then you meet the bend of a broad path, go up to the left and reach the ridge again on a col. Go through a gate and from now on avoid going into the dense wood. Go uphill north-westwards, keeping right across a firebreak, to the highest point of **Monte dei Cervi**. There's an amazing view on the top here, especially of the coast to the west of Sicily. Go left on the extensive summit plateau, once deer pasture, and begin a leisurely descent to the south. A channel runs along the right hand side.

Proceed above it and to the left of a rib of rock until you can see below the gentle pastures of Contrada Cervi. Go down towards them on the left of the ridge and continue along a path which becomes clearer later on, as far as a large water trough. The path continues to the hut below Cozzo Vituro, where you cross over the path No. 23.

Behind the hut descend along the fall-line to the start of the **Padella**, already visible. A magnificent spectacle welcomes you. It's a good idea to try and look for the way out of the pan above a little wood to the south-east on the opposite rock faces.

As you carry on you can see Polizzi above. Now the path descends to the right. A rib of rock runs below. Go on the right of it towards the Padella rock faces, then round this rib to the left towards the next scree slope. Balance downhill over enormous boulders. Do not go too far right! You come to the edge of a little valley and descend along the edge until you see a black hose pipe. Round a large boulder you make for two other large rocks on the far side and cross the densely overgrown stream. You can only get across the stream at this point.

Once you've arrived at the large rocks on the other side you can see a gap on the right in the rock face, the way out of the Padella. A well-trodden path goes in this direction through an oak wood which you could see from a distance. On the rock face you find another black hose pipe and you climb up into the gap. Up on the stony plateau, go left. Do not descend!

Slightly uphill to the east you come in 20 mins. past the upper edge of a little valley. When you reach the small road go along this through the opening in a cross fence, past the gorge of hell, to arrive at the **Vivaio Forestale**.

The way out of the Padella lies above the holm oak wood which you can already see from a distance (on the right).

20 Pizzo Carbonara, 1979m

On the roof of the Madonie

Ostello della Gioventù – rib of rock – Pizzo Carbonara

Locations: Isnello, Petralia Sottana.
Starting point: Ostello della Gioventù, 1519m. From Isnello via Portella Colla and from Petralia via Piano Battaglia on the provincial road SP 54, park before the drive up to the Ostello.
Walking times: Ostello – rib of rock 1 hr., rib of rock – P. Carbonara ¾ hr., return 1½ hrs.; total time 3¼ hrs.
Ascent: 470m.
Grade: the route (No. 2) is still not completely waymarked. The last section up to the summit is unmarked. Take note of the return route on the way up. Be careful in fog!
Food and accommodation: numerous hotels in Petralia Sottana and all along the SP 54. See also Walks 17 and 18.

The typical limestone formations of the Madonie are nowhere so clearly defined as on the Pizzo Carbonara massif. A lunar landscape with crater-like dolines extends from all sides up to the summit regions. Even if it is just under the 2000m mark, the second highest mountain of Sicily offers wide-ranging views over the island.

Go from the **Ostello della Gioventù** along the tarmac road down towards Isnello and just before the next bend in the road bear right onto the hiking path (No. 2). At the following right-hand turn-off go straight on and in the north you can see the coast. Below you on the left are situated the holiday homes of Piano Zucchi by the side of a small lake. Further on the path crosses the slope northwards. A rocky rib becomes visible which runs down the slope. There are some enormous solitary beech trees in front. The stony path goes uphill where you find lots of fossils. At the next two turn-offs go left and towards the **rip of rock**. Meanwhile the views from the left increase in splendour: the craggy west of Sicily is visible across the broad Himera valley, with Monte S. Calógero in the foreground, and on the left of it, the M. dei Cervi massif. Go through an area of beech wood where the path levels out. You come past the top of a valley (on the left) with huge beech trees and then to an 'amphitheatre'. On the right you can see the summit slope and on the left a mountain top. Head towards a col in between and round a wide left-hand bend. Hiking path No. 6 begins just before the col, in the hollow, towards Castelbuono. Go right up the broad, sparsely wooded summit slope, keeping to the fall-line and 10 mins. later cross a marked path. Taking no notice of this go straight on uphill.

A bit further on look for a way through the dwarf beech trees and when you are out in the open again, you will see Etna rising up opposite out of a sea of mountains, with your summit in front and limestone dolines in front of that. Going round it first on the right, then anti-clockwise, you climb northwards to **Pizzo Carbonara** with its iron pole and stone pyramid. Pizzo Antenna is ahead, also called Pizzo Principessa. In the south you can see across to a small hut, Bivacco Scolonazzo. Behind that M. Múfara with the ski areas of Piano Battaglia. Further right M. San Salvatore, Monte dei Cervi and then a gentle hilly landscape. Mountains have even been thrown into the Tyrrhenian sea: the Aeolian islands!

Return on the same path back to the **Ostello della Gioventù**.

The ancient landscape on the Carbonara massif.

21 Vallone della Trigna

The dolines of the Carbonara massif and the holly trees of Castelbuono

Well – Ovile Trigna – Doline Circio – Croce dei Monticelli – Cozzo Luminario – Piano Pomo – Rifo. Crispi – Contrada Castagna

Locations: Isnello and Castelbuono.

Starting point: from the well above Isnello, 640m. Coming from Castelbuono or Cefalù take the turn-off to Isnello and Collesano and go 1.5km as far as the third left-hand turn-off. Ascend steeply up the broad tarmac road and after 500m park near some villas at the well.

Walking times: well – scree slope 1 hr., scree slope – Ovile 1½ hrs., Ovile – D. Circio ¾ hr., D. Circio – C. Luminario ¾ hr., C. Luminario – Rifo. Crispi ¾ hr., Rifo. Crispi – Contrada Castagna 1¼ hrs.; total time 6 hrs.

Ascent: 1100m in ascent, 850m in descent.

Grade: the distance, terrain partly without paths and steep slopes through the Valle Trigna with a rocky section make this hike a demanding one. Route finding is difficult in fog. From Doline Circio marked with wooden boards (No. 6). Descent along a nature trail and a forest road.

Food and accommodation: Rifo. Crispi (dormitories, book in advance, tel: 0921/672279). Hotel at the end of the walk. Bars, restaurants, hotel, rooms for rent and *agriturismo* in Castelbuono.

NB: there's no public transport from your destination to Isnello and the road is arduous after the long hike.

As a hut guest in the Rifo. Crispi you can organise a lift at a reduced rate. The same applies to hotels and other accommodations.

In spite of its limestone character the Carbonara massif to the south and east is gently undulating. To the north and west the mountains have more of an Alpine character with their steep slopes and precipices. This demanding hike through the Trigna valley goes across the rocky north side littered with dolines towards the gentle wooded expanses of the east side.

Continue from the **well** a short way along the tarmac road. From here you can see down into the Vallone Chiuso and above this the cleft of the Trigna valley which is flanked by steep rock faces. The scree slope on the right, the rock step above and the path there, are the 'key points' of this walk. Go left on the bend and down the track, which is reinforced at the start, to the Chiuso stream. After that go uphill to the pasture area. At the end of the track you come past two huts (the second one is on the right above you). Be careful: walk another few minutes along the obvious path which runs parallel to the steep slopes. Shortly before this descends go to the right. Well-trodden paths go through dense vegetation to a pasture fence with an opening (remember to close it behind you!). Now head for the scree slope and – it's best to keep right – start the strenuous ascent. In the upper part of the scree slope keep right over huge boulders and reach green pastures again at the foot of the steep rock wall. Go close to the wall here up a path (right). Cross the wall over a band of rock and climb up a rock projection. After this section it gets easier again and the view over Isnello and Pizzo Dipilo puts the scree slope out of your mind. Between ancient huge holm oaks and wild pear trees make use of the tracks to reach the **Ovile Trigna**. Here there's a spring and with a bit of luck you will meet shepherds preparing Ricotta.

The path goes to the right of their hut and winds up to a col where you come to a boundary fence. Climb up the scree slope along the rocks on the right. Go up left a little way beside the fence and you will see an enormous tree standing in a large circular pasture.

The Carbonara massif is dotted with limestone dolines which are created by the effects of water. This **Doline Circio** is by far the most beautiful.

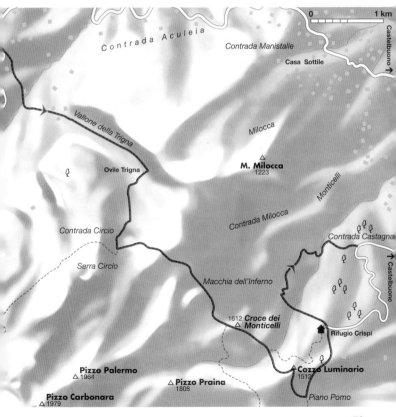

Climb up the scree slope along the rocks on the right.

The path goes across the hollow up to the opposite side and joins the marked path No. 6. Right goes round Pizzo Carbonara to Piano Battaglia, but you go up left and with every step the view to the west becomes more amazing: you see Isnello and M. San Calógero rising up behind P. Dipilo. The coast towards Palermo is visible beyond. At a height of 1600m you climb up and down past other dolines to the east where Mount Etna rises like a hovering cone. The path widens out and now goes past several crosses which adorn the various hill tops. The second stands on the right above you, the third you can already see from a distance; on the left of it, way down in the valley, you catch sight of the Rifo. Crispi.

On the hill of this cross you leave the path and go towards the refuge. Castelbuono below in the valley, Pollina on the opposite cone as well as the Aeolian islands, S. Mauro Castelverde and wide areas of the Nebrodi are all visible from here. First go a short way along the ridge to the fourth cross, **Croce dei Monticelli**, then descend right to a limestone hollow. Here, through a little wood you come to another doline. From there the forest road goes down left to the Rifo. Crispi, but you go up to the fifth cross on the **Cozzo Luminario**.

Continue downhill through an opening in the fence along the 'Sentiero Natura'. Through a wood of oaks and beech trees several hundred years old, you eventually arrive at a botanical rarity. Some enormous holly trees have survived from the last Ice Age and are today the largest in the whole of Italy.

When you come out of the wood walk over soft green pastures, **Piano Pomo**, to a wooden gate with a ladder and beyond it on the left, through another gate. Immediately afterwards descend right, cross the slope, go over the forest road again and eventually reach the **Rifo. Crispi** at Piano Sempria (accommodation).

When you arrive at the tarmac road descend for a few minutes until you meet a broad forest road on the left. Take this road now through a marvellous wood, keeping right at every turn-off, and through three wooden gates. There's an ascent to finish with: 20 minutes up along the forest road as far as the tarmac road in the **Contrada Castagna**. The road goes left via S. Guglielmo (guest house) to Castelbuono (about 8km). 3 mins. to the right brings you to a hotel.

You enter the holm oak wood after the crux move.

22 Croce dei Monticelli, 1650m

An outstanding nature trail

Rifugio Crispi – Piano Pomo – Croce dei Monticelli – Rifugio Crispi

Location: Castelbuono.
Starting point: Rifugio Crispi, 1260m. From Castelbuono take the SS 286 to Geraci Sículo and go right, almost at the end of the village, following the signposts. Past the Hotel Milocca you come to the Rifo. Crispi at Piano Sempria (11km).
Walking times: Rifugio – Piano Pomo ½ hr., P. Pomo – Croce dei Monticelli 1¼ hrs., Croce dei Monticelli – Rifo. Crispi 1¼ hrs.; total time 3 hrs.
Ascent: 400m.
Grade: easy walk on sign-posted nature trail and forest roads.
Food and accommodation: see Walk 21.

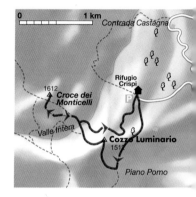

There are the most beautiful forests in Sicily in the area around Castelbuono, and thanks to the environmental protection initiative by the Parco delle Madonie they are still intact. On this walk you meet the finest oak trees, the tallest beech trees and the oldest holly trees.

At Piano Sempria, below the **Rifugio Crispi**, the path keeps to the right past a board showing a hiking map into the wood. It winds uphill and crosses the forest road (with chain). You come past various observation points. After 20 mins. the view opens out to the left and you can see Etna in the east. S. Mauro Castelverde clings to the slopes high above the Pollino valley. The Madonie are visible in the south and Monte Ferro in the foreground with the aerials. Continue uphill and reach the forest road (right is the return path to the Rifo. Crispi) and go left through the wooden gate to **Piano Pomo**. A shepherds' hut, Pagghiaru, stands on this marvellous plateau. It is covered with branches and leaves in typical fashion and has been restored for visitors. On the right through a gate there's a path marked with posts through a unique wood of holly trees – having survived from the last Ice Age and covering an area of hundreds of square metres. Then you come through a beech wood in which huge sturdy beech trees have spread out their weird roots. Another viewpoint awaits you at **Cozzo Luminario** – the typical landscape of Pizzo Carbonara and its foothills, bare, stony, and with limestone hollows. Solitary holm oaks grow on the slopes. From the cross you can see Castelbuono far below and the little village of Pollina above on a pyramid, to the left of it Monte S. Giovanni with the Gibilmanna sanctuary, and behind that the Tyrrhenian sea with the Aeolian islands. You can see two crosses on a stony ridge. You will climb up to the second cross. The path first descends into the limestone hollow below. (Right is the return path.) Go straight on through a little wood and over verdant pastures and then up to the left. You come through a wooden gate to the marked path No. 6 where you bear right uphill. On the hill of the second cross you leave the path to the right. When you arrive at the **Croce dei Monticelli** you can see the beautiful forest of Castelbuono, Monte Milocca and the Rifo. Crispi.

After taking a rest on the summit go back along the same path to the limestone hollow. You now go below C. Luminario downhill to the left, meet the forest road and go to the right. About ¼ hr. later you take a left turn-off (right goes to Piano Pomo). Walk along the forest road, which is not open to traffic, through a mixed forest for about ½ hr. as far as a chain and then left along the nature trail back to the **Rifugio Crispi**.

The meadows below 'Monticelli', limestone hollows with verdant pastures.

23 Monte Macabubbo, 1204m

The local mountains of Isnello

I Pianetti – Monte Grotta Grande – Pozzo di Puraccia – Monte Macabubbo – I Pianetti

Locations: Isnello, Gratteri.
Starting point: I Pianetti, 834m. From Cefalù towards Isnello. Past the Santuario Gibilmanna, right at the turn-off to Gratteri and 1.9km to the parking bay on the left.
Walking times: I Pianetti – M. Grotta Grande 1¼ hrs., M. Grotta Grande – Pozzo di Puraccia ¾ hr., Pozzo di Puraccia – M. Macabubbo ½ hr., M. Macabubbo – I Pianetti 1 hr.; total time 3½ hrs.
Ascent: 460m.
Grade: easy walk, but only partly marked up to now (No. 12, wooden posts with little boards). Be careful in fog.
Food and accommodation: hotels and huts from Isnello to Piano Battaglia. Bars in Isnello and rooms for rent in Gratteri. See also Walk 21.
NB: it's worth making a visit to the Gibilmanna sanctuary and doing the walk to Pizzo S. Angelo (760m), not only because of the fantastic view across wide areas of the coast. The Benedictine monastery which was destroyed by the Saracens in the 12th century has been rebuilt and extended over the years. It has many interesting things to see from this era. It is located in the B zone of the Parco delle Madonie and since quite recently has housed information on the protection of the forest.

Isnello, on the river of the same name, lies sheltered at the foot of steep limestone cliffs. If you are looking at the village from a long way off you can see a yawning black hole in the rock face. Since the Middle Ages the village has lain spread out directly below around the castle which was once a feudal castle and is today in ruins. A bridge in the northern part of the village with a water trough for the donkey caravans (Italian asino) was previously called Asinara. The name Isnello developed from that.

From the car park **I Pianetti**, a sign points to the 'Sentiero No. 12' and to Monte Grotta Grande. A wild and craggy landscape on the right and a beautiful panorama on the left (from M. Sant'Angelo as far as the wooded slopes of the Carbonara massif) indicate the start of this walk. The narrow track crosses the flower-covered slope parallel to the rocks. Star anemones and yellow asphodel, vivid red wild spring roses and spurge flourish here. After ½ hr. you reach a small light wood above a gully with pendunculate and holm oaks. The path gets rather lost and then after the first group of trees on the right goes uphill.You see Monte Grotta Grande opposite and from a col, a little further on, Pizzo Carbonara on the left as well. The path goes above a steep valley past a shepherds' hut with a sheep pen and continues to ascend past some wild pear trees which have a lovely white blossom early in the year. You come to a boundary fence. Before going through the opening, ascend left to the cross on **Monte Grotta Grande**. Be careful! The rock face drops down vertically to Isnello which spreads out below with its red

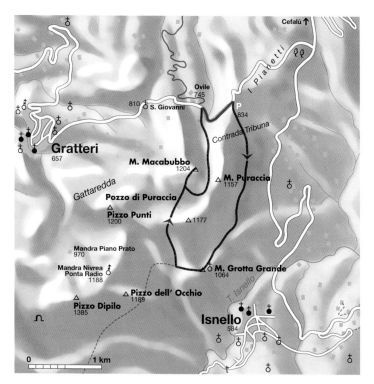

roofs. Directly underneath there's a cave in the wall. When you return to the gap in the fence continue to along the main path. M. Puraccia is on the right and Pizzo Dipilo on the left. Hiking path No. 12 descends here, swings to the left and carries on to Isnello, but you leave this path and go above a fence and parallel to it, until you reach the upper part of a small valley. Here, climb up right. Shortly afterwards this valley ends at a plateau. Shepherds have laboriously piled up the stones to create more pastures in this barren landscape. Cross over this plain and go up to a ridge. At the top you are surprised by a large alpine meadow below, Pozzo di Puraccia, which lies at the foot of M. Macabubbo on the right opposite. The view to the left is to the sea and on the right you can see M. Sant'Angelo again through a notch. The return route goes through this notch. But first of all you descend to the **Pozzo di Puraccia** meadow. At the hut on the right you first head towards the

Isnello and the local mountain, M. Macabubbo, can be seen best from the Trigna valley.

round sheep pens above, then to a green ramp and eventually right to the broad summit of **Monte Macabubbo**. From here you can see the coast in the distance, the village of Gratteri below in the valley and the starting point of the walk. A dramatic landscape frames the deep valley through which you will be descending. The whole of the Madonie as far as the Nebrodi mountains are visible in the south and east. Go back downhill to the meadow and take an obvious path left to the notch (1130m). Further on you come past a water trough which stands below the summit. Wild serrated rocks tower up above. From here the valley basin widens out with steep rock precipices. The path goes past another water trough across verdant pastures, enormous boulders and a small stream. First you are on the right of it, then you cross over to the left, and traverse the slope. You can see the car parked on the road and below, a large water trough on a green flat area. An obvious path takes you there. When you arrive, keep left going downhill and reach a broad path which leads to the road at a farm. Return along the road to the right in 10 mins. to the starting point **I Pianetti**.

A view of Isnello vertically down from M. Grotta Grande.

The west

Fiume Imera forms the border between west and east Sicily. The watershed is to be found just under 40km inland at Tre Monzelli. The source of the Imera Meridionale is here. It then joins the **Fiume Salso** which eventually flows into the Mediterranean at **Licata** in the Golfo di Gela. The west, the rather unstable part of the Sicilian triangle with the name **Val di Mazara**, does not have a continuous range of mountains. The mountain peaks rise up singly or in groups from gentle slopes. Valleys or plains lie in between. While the north is dominated principally by limestone, the **Monti Sicani** in the south tend to consist more of sandstone and gypsum. The contrast between overdeveloped conurbations and idyllic sleepy countryside could not be greater than in the west of the island.

To the west of the Himera river there's a country road leading to the small village of **Sciara** with a superb view of the Madonie. Here in December they celebrate the festival of the Immacolata with a torch-light procession. At sunrise young men jump over piles of blazing torches. A breath of Aryan custom – as usual – has reached here. From Cáccamo you reach **Ventimiglia** across the dam of the **Fiume S. Leonardo** and small mountain roads. The steep **Monti di Calamagna** tower up above. Lots of small settlements lie scattered here, amongst them **Cefalà Diana** with the remains of a castle fortification, and Godrano at the 'bastion' of the Busambra. Beyond this limestone wall you come to **Corleone**, at the edge of Monti Sicani. It's pleasant to travel southwards along the small winding roads and through the isolated villages into the province of Agrigento. The landscape is tinged white and pink with the almond blossom in February, the air is clear, there are views over to the Madonie and Etna and the climate is pleasantly mild for hiking. During carnival time when there are relatively few tourists about, one festival follows another. Driving westwards through the gypsum landscape you discover hidden treasures: north of **Sambuca** the archaeological excavations of Monte Adranone from the 6 BC and at **Contessa Entellina**, the wonderful monastery church of Sta. Maria del Bosco. **Gibellina** has lain in ruins since an earthquake. The new town has become a work shop for modern art. To the south, at **S. Ninfa**, a guided walk through the limestone caves of the same name provides revealing information about the geology of the Sicanian mountains. **Marsala** marks the most western point of Sicily at the sea. The town was one of the most important trade settlements of the Phoenicians in the western Mediterranean. To the north of it, at **Mozia**, you can visit the salt works with a WWF guide and take a trip to the **Égadi islands**. From the harbour town of **Trápani** it's only a hop, skip and a jump to **Erice**. Opinions differ about whether it can outdo Taormina in being the most beautiful town in Sicily. The long-distance path, **'Sentiero Italia'**, starts (or finishes) here. The **Monti di Trápani** have been quarried for marble since 1960. The 'Perlato di Sicilia' is even exported. Meanwhile the quarrying activity sustains the surrounding community. You can look eastwards on all the walks towards the **Golfo di Castellammare** and you will never get tired of the view. The archaeological area of **Segesta** is situated to the south. Hikes lead through the surrounding valleys up to the theatre situated on a hill. As you walk towards the gulf your gaze falls on the 1046m high **Monte Inici**. A steep forest road ends in an amazingly beautiful panorama from the summit. The **Monti di Conca d'Oro** surround the town and bay of Palermo. They stand on their own or in small groups like guardians watching over the villages on their slopes and the unexpected cultural and scenic treasures. Now and then the hiker will find fossils at the side of the path in these mountains. So it's not hard to imagine that they were mostly below sea level millions of years ago.

Almond blossom in the south (Monte Conca, Walk 37).

24 Monte San Calógero, 1326m

Guardians of the Himera plain

Santa Nicola – Rocca Fera – Monte San Calógero

Location: Cáccamo.

Starting point: Sta. Nicola, 630m. From the motorway exit Términi Imerese along the SS 285 to Cáccamo (9km). At the petrol station as you come into the town go left along the ring road (Circonvallazione) in the direction of Roccapalumba. After 3km (the road goes downhill), before the ring road joins the through road, go up steeply to the left. The road leads past a new housing estate. At the fork follow the right-hand road for 1½km as far as the small hamlet of Sta. Nicola.

Walking times: Sta. Nicola – Sta. Maria 1 hr., Sta. Maria – Rocca Fera ¾ hr., Rocca Fera – M. San Calógero ¾ hr.,

return 2 hrs.; total time 4½ hrs.

Ascent: 700m.

Grade: easy walk, but hardly marked, and for a short way without paths. Rocky terrain in the upper area.

Food and accommodation: bars, restaurants and hotel in Cáccamo. *Agriturismo* in Sciara (east of Cáccamo).

NB: the festival of 'Castellana Mediterranea', lasting several days, takes place every year in the first week in September.

During the week the elected Lady of Cáccamo castle and her entourage wear traditional costumes and recreate music and splendour of the 14th century.

The broad Himera valley, also called Fiume Grande now, separates the Madonie from the western Sicilian mountains. The first noticeable elevation west of the Torrente Imera is the beautifully formed Monte San Calógero, named after the hermit who retreated there. The Sicilian Greeks called him Eurako and in 649 BC founded the town of Himera on its eastern slope. Huge megalithic walls lie in the region of Cortevecchia. The Carthaginians destroyed the part of the town on the Himera river. To the west of the mountain pyramid they erected a fortress, amongst other things, and the Normans built a castle on the ruins which they continued to extend several times. Today it dominates the town of Cáccamo.

From **Sta. Nicola** follow the ascending tarmac road. It becomes a flat unsurfaced road. Your summit is on the right ahead of you and you go past

The walk starts in the Contrada Sta. Nicola.

a turn-off on the left at a pylon. The path gently descends from here. The coast and part of the town of Términi Imerese emerge in the north-west. The **Contrada Sta. Maria** farm is below on the pastures. At the next turn-off, the track swings to the left and you bear right along a broad path which, 5 mins. later, ends at some rocks. An obvious path continues straight on. Go up here on the right behind the rocks to the top and head for the holm oak wood. Many goat paths lead to the wood (animal tracks) and in places they join into one broad stony path. Always keeping to the right you come past a water trough and you can see across to the summit region. Rocca Fera towers up from the pastures in the fall-line. You reach the far side of the Rocca Fera round a big left hand bend: from the trough numerous well-trodden paths lead up to it. Again keep to the track furthest right. Climb steeply up through the forest and reach a plateau. The ridge which you have been walking parallel to, ends on the right at M. dell'Uomo and M. S. Nicasio which together become this plateau. Go to the left and find at the foot of the summit slope, ribs of rock with red arrows pointing to the left.

Following these you come to a point above **Rocca Fera** which stands below you on the left and seems a small elevation now. From this col you zigzag up between the rocks and go left again to a ramp. This crosses the slope to the right and is reinforced with dry-stone walls. The path winds up to the summit of **Monte San Calógero** where there are some aerials with solar panels. There's an extensive view to the west: Capo Zafferano and Capo Gallo with their rock formations enclose the Gulf of Palermo. Conca d'Oro and the whole hinterland is visible. The Calamigna mountains are an imposing sight with the conspicuous notch between Pizzo Canna and Serra del Leone. Rocca Busambra with Bosco di Ficuzza can be seen to the south. In the east, in the distant Himera valley, numerous villages and hamlets lie on the slopes. The mountain ranges of Madonie tower up above with the strikingly huge Carbonara massif. On the slopes below, on M. Castellaccio, you can see the Cyclopean stones with which, presumably, the town wall of ancient Himera was built. Above the estuary of the Torrente Imera you can make out the uncovered site of the temple.

Go a few paces to the north and look down steeply to the overdeveloped coastline at Términi Imerese. It's hard to imagine that at one time the spas of ancient Himera were located here: '… nymphs created them to give Hercules some refreshment on his homeward journey …' The spas have in the meantime been turned into modern thermal baths.

Return along the same path after a rest on the summit.

The coast in the west with the prominent rocks of Capo Zafferano, M. Pellegrino and M. Gallo.

25 Pizzo di Casa, 1211m

The 'local mountain' of Mezzojuso

Mezzojuso – mountain chapel 'Madonna dell'Udienza' – Pizzo di Casa – Contrada Cerasa – Mezzojuso

Location: Mezzojuso.
Starting point: Piazza Umberto I. On the SS 121, Palermo – Agrigento, as far as the Mezzojuso exit. Along the mountain road to the centre.
Walking times: Mezzojuso – mountain chapel ½ hr., mountain chapel – P. di Casa 1 hr., P. di Casa – C. Cerasa 1 hr., C. Cerasa – mountain chapel 1¼ hrs., moun-

tain chapel – Mezzojuso ¼ hr.; total time 4 hrs.
Ascent: 700m.
Grade: the walk is easy, with short sections without paths. Waymarkers only at the start through the forest (red).
Food and accommodation: bars, pizzeria in Mezzojuso. Hotel in Bolognetta. *Agriturismo* in Godrano.

In Sicily there are five mountain villages which were founded in the 14th century by immigrants from Albania. Apart from Piana degli Albanesi, the language of the Albanians has been lost in Palazzo Adriano, Contessa Entellina, Sta. Cristina Gela and Mezzojuso. The Greek orthodox church in Mezzojuso celebrates a festival of bread on the 6th December, on St. Nicholas' day. Devout Catholics are not to be outdone and celebrate a similar festival on the 19th March, the day of S. Giuseppe. Old and young, everyone is involved in the two festivals.

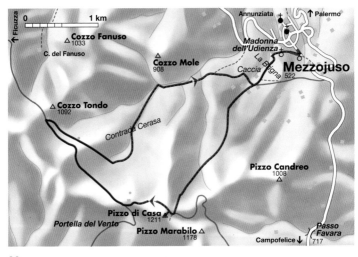

The rocks above Contrada Cerasa. The small village of Cefalà Diana and the coast in the background.

The road into the centre of **Mezzojuso** brings you to the Piazza Umberto I. At the end of the Piazza on the left, at the corner of a narrow street, you see a marble shrine with an image of the Madonna carved in relief. Go steeply up the little cobbled street. Yellow signs point the way to the mountain chapel of **'Madonna dell'Udienza'**. Up some steps of the same name you pass by the chapel and reach a gate under an eucalyptus tree. Go beyond it towards a villa, turn left and follow an unsurfaced road for 10 mins. as far as a conspicuous left-hand bend. On the right there's a farm. Here bear right from the little street, go up through the forest along a path and come to the end of a road with several gates. You will be returning through the right hand one. Go a few paces along the road to the left and take a broad forest path opposite. The path, originally well-made (red waymarkers), leads through a marvellous chestnut wood past an *azienda* and becomes more and more stony. In a clearing take the middle broader path straight on to a plateau. You will see P. di Casa ahead. Further up, ascend round to the right towards the rocks, then parallel to them in a southerly direction (some shepherds' huts on the right). After the next platform, on the upper pastures, leave the marked route which bears right to an observation tower. Without any paths head towards the col below P. di Casa. P. Candreo lies on the left. There are wide areas of ivy on the right at the foot of the steep slope and opposite you can see the steep rock faces of M. Marabilo with the old quarries to which there's a little road leading up from the left. First head towards the quarry and then you'll find an obvious path on the right which takes you uphill. You then curve round to the left up to the highest point of **Pizzo di Casa**. You can see the sea beyond Cefalà Diana with the Castello and Villafrati, Pizzo Leone and M. S. Calógero in the north-east and the Madonie in the distance. The curve spans the fertile hills in the south as far as the immediate western area where you can see the rocky Rocca Busambra. The fire-watchtower stands below on Portella del Vento.

From the summit descend the rib of rock, go left and on the other side of a pasture fence continue along an unsurfaced road to the watchtower. Just before it bear left and where the road divides go right, practically on the level, in the direction of Rocca Busambra. On the right below is the **Contrada Cerasa** with a marvellous mixed forest and the path you will be following later on. 20 mins. from the watchtower leave the forest road which leads to the Bosco di Ficuzza and veer off left downhill. Past a firebreak continue along the right hand path. Just afterwards you will find a well (water channel) with a beautiful view over to Pizzo di Casa. ¼ hr. after the well the path descends. A large flat clearing has left no signs of a path. Head left towards the bizarre rocky landscape and the forest below and go downhill. Eventually the two firebreaks join up. A spring and dense vegetation make the route finding difficult. On the left of the water course the path comes to a clearing. There's an old mill here. Go straight down. The path becomes rocky and steep and you walk along a ridge between the two streams. Where they meet, cross the water to the right. Two uphill climbs bring you to a rocky section. Be careful: a path here descends left to the road, but you climb up over two rocky ledges and afterwards, keeping at the same height, cross the woody slope. 10 mins. later you come to a field. Follow the fence on the right until you come to a house on the other side. Go through a gate past the house, go onto the road through a wooden gate and turn left along the path where you started the walk, back to **Mezzojuso**.

The path takes a big sweep round to the left through the Contrada Cerasa valley basin. M. S. Calógero and the Madonie in the background.

26 Round Rocca Ramusa, 1209m

At the edge of the Bosco di Ficuzza

Ficuzza – Fonte Ramusa – col – Fonte Ramusa – Ficuzza

The view looking back: Rocca Busambra and the Madonie.

Location: Ficuzza.
Starting point: castle square in Ficuzza, 683m. On the SS 624, Palermo – Sciacca, Altofonte exit, then to Ficuzza.
Walking times: Ficuzza – Fonte Ramusa ½ hr., Fonte Ramusa – col 1 hr., col – track ½ hr., track – Ficuzza 1 hr.; total time 3 hrs.
Ascent: 530m.
Grade: not difficult, runs partly over terrain without paths and requires a good sense of direction. No waymarkers.
Food and accommodation: bar, *trattoria*, Rifugio Alpe Cucco (restaurant, rooms) in Ficuzza. *Agriturismo* in Godrano.

Rocca Busambra with its steep north face looks like a desolate rambling massif from a distance. Its western corner, however, is a mountain world all by itself with magnificent peaks and narrow valleys.

From the castle square in **Ficuzza** take the road on the left at the left-hand side of the castle which curves to the right on its way out of the village. After 10 mins. bear right at a turn-off onto the unsurfaced road in the direction of 'Alpe Ramusa'. Just after a cosy little picnic area you reach **Fonte Ramusa**. On the right below there's a large building and a water trough. After the following left-hand bend you leave the road through a gap in the fence, go uphill on the right of a water container and along the edge of a long field enclosed by a wood towards the rock faces. On the right you meet an obvious path and go through a strip of wood to the next field. Afterwards you enter a dense forest. The path swings into the right hand valley between high rock faces and becomes stony. Go uphill, cross over the forest boundary and after that come to a **col** below **Rocca Ramusa** (its highest point is on the right above). A narrow wildly overgrown valley extends in the west and on the horizon you can see the area around M. Iato. Go left from the col, and continue beyond a fence along well-trodden paths. A stony, barren plateau opens up before you with solitary holm oaks. Many rare species of Ophrys grow here in spring. Descend right and find an opening in the middle of a pasture fence. Go behind it and walk to the right beside the fence. At the edge of the plain, below the outlying rocks, there are some ruins of former stone houses. First descend left in front of these, then keeping diagonally right, you come to a pasture fence at the edge of a plateau. Slip through the gap in the fence where the path finishes. The rocks of Rocca Ramusa protrude into the valley. At the end of the valley there's a farm house. Continue along the fence to the left until you see on the right, below on the valley floor, a path and a hut.

Begin your descent to the right here and find a narrow firebreak between the dense blackberry bushes. On the right of the hut (with cisterns) head towards the rock faces and reach a road which leads gently uphill to the left below the north walls of R. Ramusa. You see Ficuzza on the left and later Rocca Busambra. Past a cattle trough you go through two gates in the space of 10 mins. You have to find your way ahead across fields and round clumps of trees until you see on the left below, the big house at **Fonte Ramusa**. Continue to the road and return to the castle square in **Ficuzza**.

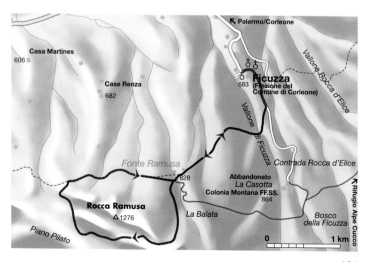

27 Rocca Busambra, 1613m

A limestone 'bastion' above the Bosco della Ficuzza

Rifo. Alpe Cucco – Piano della Tramontana – Rocca Busambra – Rifo. Alpe Cucco

Location: Ficuzza.
Starting point: Rifugio Alpe Cucco, 945m. As in Walk 26 to Ficuzza, then 5½km (2km of it is surfaced) to the Rifo. Alpe Cucco, park there.
Walking times: Rifo. Alpe Cucco – P. d. Tramontana 1 hr., P. d. Tramontana – Rocca Busambra 1½ hrs., return 2 hrs.; total time 4½ hrs.
Ascent: 680m.
Grade: without paths along the ridge and on the summit slope. Sure-footedness, good sense of direction and fitness essential. Only recommended in clear visibility.
Food and accommodation: see Walk 26.

The huge wall of Rocca Busambra protects the luxuriant Ficuzza wood from the scorching southern sun like a bastion. It is frequently covered in a cap of cloud and the locals have found a mystical explanation for this in a legend. A merciless hermit once lived in a grotto on Busambra. One day a sick woman was going on a pilgrimage to Marineo to the Madonna della Dajna. Dying of thirst she asked the hermit for some water, but he refused. On her return journey she found, instead of the grumpy hermit, a cap of cloud overhead. This damp good fortune has stayed ever since and keeps the surrounding area fresh.

Go from the **Rifo. Alpe Cucco** back to the road, then left, past a turn-off on the left and straight on along the gently ascending road. After ½ hr. you come to a hill-top at a boundary fence (sign: 'Cerasa'). The road here goes downhill. Pizzo di Casa is opposite and Portella del Vento in front with a fire-watchtower. After the opening in the fence go immediately right and leave the road through a gate into the wood. The path, broad at first, ascends to a rounded hilltop. Shortly afterwards go right along an obvious path up the slope. Through a gully with porphyry-red soil you come to **Piano della Tramontana**, an extensive high pasture (make note of the link to the gully for the return!). A gentle mountain ridge stretches out in front of you. Climb up without paths to its highest point, continue westwards along the ridge until Rocca Busambra comes into view. The whole of the ridge (your ascent route), the summit in the far distance and the gentle incline of the southern slope of Busambra (your return) are all visible from here. When you arrive on a col there's an even more stunning view down across the towering rock face opposite. You reach the gentle summit slope through a gate. The path straight on is your return. Go uphill to the right here to reach the crest (be careful!) where you clamber up and down, in places on the left of the ridge, to the summit of **Rocca Busambra**. At this point the path goes to a hollow, past an information board and continues to the next rise where there's a trig point. Ficuzza wood, the village itself and the Alpe Cucco lie below. Between the surrounding villages, at the foot of the Calamigna mountains, Cefalà Diana is clearly visible with the castle. In the east lie Etna and the Madonie and in the west the mountains of the lato valley. The craggy bulk of Rocca Ramusa can be seen ahead.

For the return go a short way back along the ridge. There's a farm in the south, way below in the valley. Descend in this direction for just under 50m. Then, only slightly losing height, parallel to the ridge and past a limestone hollow, continue along an obvious path diagonally to the east along the path you could see from your ascent. You come to the notch and the path you came on. Return along this to the **Rifo. Alpe Cucco**.

Ascending the ridge (Rocca Ramusa in the background).

28 Ficuzza wood

The royal hunting ground

Ficuzza – Quattro Finaite – Pulpito del Re – Pizzo Castrateria – Ficuzza

Location: Ficuzza.
Starting point: see Walk 26.
Walking times: Ficuzza – Quattro Finaite 1 hr., Quattro Finaite – Pulpito del Re ½ hr., Pulpito del Re – Pizzo Castrateria ¼ hr., Pizzo Castrateria – Ficuzza 1 hr.; total time 2¾ hrs.
Ascent: 250m.
Grade: a peaceful walk, for the most part on broad paths, waymarkers (red and white, and yellow and green).
Food and accommodation: see Walk 26.

During the Napoleonic invasion of Italy, at the beginning of the 19th century, the Bourbon King Ferdinand IV fled from Naples and for more than five years found peace and quiet in Sicily, a second title together with crown, and extensive forest land with rich fauna for his favourite pastime which was hunting. Then, as Ferdinand I, king of Sicily, he had two excellent hunting grounds: La Favorita, the green lungs of Palermo still existing today, and Bosco di Ficuzza where there were wolves, wild pigs, deer and foxes. Ficuzza wood is today a protected wood run by the state forestry.

In **Ficuzza** at the Piazza go left below the castle, past a pizzeria as far as a cross-road. On the opposite side (red and white waymarkers) you come to a broad flight of steps which lead down beside some wooden railings and join a tarmac road round a left-hand bend. Through a gap in the fence on the other side you come to the old railway station of Ficuzza, go round the tower and continue along the disused railway track to the right. Through an overgrown wood of oaks and ash trees you pass the Vallone Rocca d'Elice (your return path). On the right there's a water container. A path goes downhill to the left at a turn-off. The track goes straight ahead into a tunnel. Leave the track here to the right and climb up parallel to the fence. On the 'roof' of the tunnel you come to a junction, **Quattro Finaite**. The tarmac road connects Godrano with Marineo, the unsurfaced road ('Sentiero Italia') leads through an iron gate to the Val dei Conti. Go right following the green and yellow posts. Bear left at the next turn-off. On the other side of the road barrier the path ascends to a clearing (remains of a charcoal kiln). Here take the right-hand path and continue uphill to the **Pulpito del Re** which is on the left of the path. The 'king's seat' was hewn out of crystalline sandstone. The limestone of Rocca Busambra once lay hidden below this sandstone and the landscape of this walk only evolved after the processes of erosion and uplift. Back on the hiking path you climb up to the **Portella Gramigna**, a ridge where you go briefly to the right. As soon as the view opens up, go downhill in the direction of the steep rock faces into a hollow and continue as far as a cross fence with a gate. Before going through, it's worth climbing up left to **Pizzo Castrateria**, 897m (5 mins. to the left parallel to the fence). The view is stunning. On the right, on the far side of the Scanzano lake, you can see Pizzuta and Cumeta at Piana degli Albanesi. The beautifully formed Ramusa is a fascinating sight in the Busambra chain on the right. Pizzo di Casa comes into view on the left and in the north M. S. Calógero and the Monti di Calamigna with a backdrop of the Madonie. Why didn't the king have his seat installed here?

Return to the path and descend beyond the gate. Then cross the slope and continue your descent through an eerie wood. Ivy entwines itself around the trunks of dead trees. There's not much left to see of the original stem of the 'strangling ivy'. Straight ahead you come to the upper reaches of the **Vallone Rocca d'Elice**. Red and white waymarkers indicate left to the Rifo. Alpe Cucco and you veer right in the direction of Ficuzza.

'Strangling ivy' in Ficuzza wood.

The path goes through the oak wood up a gentle incline along the stream to a forest road (left to Ficuzza). Continue walking through the valley: go right, over a bridge and then left into the wood. The stream is your guide. Always keeping to the right of it and after ¼ hr. you come to the water container and the railway track which you follow left to the old railway station and then go uphill to your starting point in **Ficuzza**.

29 La Pizzuta, 1333m

An Albanian minority in Sicily

Piana degli Albanesi – Portella del Garrone – Casa della Neviera – La Pizzuta – Piana degli Albanesi

Location: Piana degli Albanesi.
Starting point: Piazza Vittorio Emmanuele, 700m. On the SS 624, Palermo – Sciacca, Altofonte exit, then to Piana degli Albanesi.
Walking times: Piana degli Albanesi – Portella Garrone 1 hr., Portella Garrone – 2nd col 1 hr., summit detour ¾ hr., 2nd col – Piana degli Albanesi 1 hr.; total time 3¾ hrs.
Ascent: 633m.
Grade: partly marked paths (red and white, and yellow and green). Sure-footedness is essential over terrain without paths to the summit.
Food and accommodation: bars, restaurant and rooms for rent in Piana. Small bed and breakfast in S. Cristina Gela, east of Piana. Hotels in Palermo and Monreale.

Piana degli Albanesi was founded at the end of the 15th century by Albanian colonists. They settled in southern Italy and in Sicily to cultivate royal estates. They have kept their traditions up to the present day (language and religion).

From the Piazza in **Piana degli Albanesi**, first follow the Corso and then go left up some steps and through narrow streets out of the village. The red and white waymarkers of the 'Sentiero Italia' lead you past the ruins of the hospital and the small chapel of **S. Maria dell'Odigitria** towards the steep limestone slopes of La Pizzuta. The tarmac road is later unsurfaced and then becomes a stony path which, after a few bends, leads up to **Portella del Garrone**. From this notch you can see the pastures which extend up between La Pizzuta and Cozzo di Fratantoni. That's where you have to go uphill, but first follow the waymarkers downhill. Gradually on the right Monreale comes into view, with Castel Daccia above on a hill, and afterwards Conca d'Oro with Palermo. Take note: after 10 mins., as soon as you can see the 'Centro Maria Immacolata' close by on the right in a little wood, you come to a rounded hilltop. At a rounded peak leave the 'Sentiero Italia' which leads downhill and bear left. Take a well-trodden path for a while parallel to a pasture fence till you reach a ledge on the slope and can see some large ruins above. The walled depressions in this high plateau are former 'snow houses', **Casa della Neviera**, in which the snow was pressed to ice and transported in blocks to Palermo during the summer. When you reach the col you come across some yellow and green waymarker posts which you follow to the left. Climb over a fence and following the waymarkers you come to the next **col**. The rocky Pelavet rises up on the right. The highest point of La Pizzuta (left) is still blocked from view. You can see a narrow green gully on its slopes. Going up through this you proceed to the next slope and clamber over the rocks up to the summit of La Pizzuta. You are rewarded by a spectacular view. Rocca Busambra and Monte San Calógero are visible in the east and the north, with the Madonie in between in the distance and the fjord-like reservoir and village of Piana on the plateau below. The **descent** goes back the same way to the col. Then it follows the waymarkers to the left (east) round numerous bends down the mountain. Through a pine wood, then through two openings in the fence you meet the route again at the hospital where you started and return to **Piana degli Albanesi**.

The area surrounding Piana and the massive Rocca Busambra.

30 Pizzo Mirabella, 1165m

Through the feudal estates of the diocese of Monreale

Masseria La Chiusa – Vuscagghiera – Pizzo Mirabella – Masseria Procura – Masseria La Chiusa

Locations: S. Giuseppe Iato, S. Cipirello.
Starting point: Masseria La Chiusa, 510m. Main road Palermo – Sciacca, S. Giuseppe exit, and right along the provincial road SP 20 towards Palermo/Pioppo 3½km as far as a left-hand turn-off (signs for various hiking paths). Left here along the uneven 'SP 67 bis' for another 2km to the 'Parcheggio La Chiusa', where a barrier and an information board mark the starting point.
Walking times: Chiusa – Vuscagghiera 1½ hrs., Vuscagghiera – summit turn-off ¾ hr., summit and back ¾ hr., turn-off – Procura 1 hr., Procura – Chiusa ½ hr.; total time 4½ hrs.
Ascent: 770m.
Grade: steep ascent up to the Vuscagghiera ridge. The paths are for the most part obvious or marked (yellow and green posts). Even so, a good sense of direction is essential. The last section to the summit is over rocks.
Food and accommodation: see Walk 29.
NB: numerous easy walks are marked in the area around the Masseria La Chiusa. From Giuseppe Iato and San Cipirello there are some short hiking paths as well as a track leading to the high plateau of M. Iato and the archaeological excavations of the same name. Signs make the route finding easier. From the high plateau there's a magnificent view across the Iato valley to the Mirabella chain of mountains. The ancient settlement of Iatos which was inhabited from the 10th century BC into the Middle Ages, is of the greatest interest historically.

Masseria La Chiusa lies below the rocky Mirabella. M. della Fierra in the background.

The wide Iato valley south of Palermo is enclosed by the mountain ridges of M. Iato and Cumeta in the south, the deeply-cut massif of La Pizzuta in the east and the rocky chain of the Pizzo Mirabella mountains in the north. The valley is open to the west and the water from all the side valleys accumulates in the Fiume Iato and flows westwards into Poma lake. The abundance of this region's water is, and was for centuries, the reason for the agricultural prosperity of the Iato valley. Numerous mills, feudal farms or at least the ruins of them, sit in picturesque locations on the mountain slopes and are evidence of the time when the bishopric of Monreale gave its estates to the feudal lords as fiefdoms so that they might cultivate and inhabit the territory for protection against the Muslims.

From the car park you come in a few minutes in the direction of the traffic to the **Masseria La Chiusa**. Here take the track to the right. Up a gentle incline first head towards the rock faces, then go parallel to them to the west. Past a turn-off on the left leave the road to the right after ¼ hr. Go up along the second and higher track which you can drive on, to the right through an entrance gate until you reach a walled water container on the left. Through a gate on the left go between the wall and the field fence. Be careful: after a 3 min. ascent parallel to the fence and before the path levels out, turn sharp left and begin the steep climb up a mountain path. This leads through an oak wood below some **caves** in which prehistoric rock drawings have been discovered. At the turn-off to one of the caves go right and come to a second wood across some rocky ground. After a short crossing of the slope the path winds up to the **Vuscagghiera** notch. On the left you can see through a valley cleft to the summit. The path gets lost here in some tall grass. Go straight on in a northerly direction and slightly to the right uphill to a mountain ridge and a boundary fence. Go along the ridge on the right to a rounded peak and then change sides through a gap in the fence. Along a well-trodden path parallel to the fence you meet a broad path. Go left here. The path runs on the level at first, then down into the wood. When you are on open ground again you can see the Iato valley on the left through a cleft. At a turn-off which bears left down to a pasture, Zotta 'I Chianti, go up right until you reach a forest road. The 'Sentiero Italia' goes past here and to the right via Portella della Paglia to Piana degli Albanesi. Continue to a col. Here the 'Sentiero Italia' turns off right.

You descend left and 3 mins. later, round a conspicuous right-hand bend, you leave the forest road to the left along a mountain path in the direction of P. Mirabella. Gently descending, then ascending, the path crosses the slope and finishes shortly before a col to which you ascend along tracks up to the left. On the right you now see the rocky ridge along which you climb up to the summit of **Pizzo Mirabella**. In the area to the left of the ridge it's an easier incline to the top. Be careful! This gives you a bird's eye view of the Iato valley. The villages of San Giuseppe and San Cipirello nestle at the foot of M. Iato. Before they were exiled, Friedrich II deported thousands of rebellious Saracens onto its gentle plateau where the Greek archaeological site is to be found. Portella Ginestra separates the massifs of Cumeta and Pizzuta and is a reminder of the Mafia presence in the region since the massacre of 1.5.1947.

Carefully scramble down by the same route and return to the forest road (left below the Vallone Procura). Go downhill and leave the road on the third bend to the right. Now go straight ahead downhill, through a pine grove and over a fence. Then you cross a field and reach the track which leads right to Giacalone. Go left and past the large farm, **Brivatura**. Keep descending down the track to reach the houses of Trifiró (left of the path). Behind a pasture fence go immediately right to make a detour round the wet and overgrown track. Between derelict houses you come to a broad path and go left, directly towards P. Mirabella.

Straight on, past the overgrown track which ends here, you come to the valley cleft of V. Procura where the path swings to the right into a side valley. Through a cleft you can see the ruins of the Masseria lying in a picturesque location on a flat rock. Past an old tower go round the side valley: the path winds downhill to a stream by the side of which you descend for a short way. Then you cross the slope between steep boulders and arrive at the cleft you saw from above and the **Masseria Procura**. The corn store where tithes from the surrounding estates were once handed in, used to be situated here. Descend on the left to the road where there's a water container. Keeping left along the road, you come past your ascent route and return to the **Masseria La Chiusa**.

On the descent: looking towards the peak of Mirabella and into the Vallone Procura on the right.

31 Timpone di Caronìa, 917m

The Conca d'Oro from its most photogenic side

La Pineta – Timpone di Caronìa – Portella Sta. Anna – La Pineta

Location: San Martino delle Scale.
Starting point: La Pineta behind the cemetery, 565m. Either from Palermo via

Bocca del Falco or from Monreale to S. Martino delle Scale. From the Piazza above the church take the tarmac road 1km to the north-west up to the cemetery and continue along the dirt road to the pine grove. Park below the picnic area.
Walking times: pine grove – Timpone di Caronia 1½ hrs., Timpone di Caronia – Portella Sta. Anna ½ hr., P. Sta. Anna – pine grove ¾ hr.; total time 2¾ hrs.
Ascent: 380m.
Grade: not marked, but easy walk on obvious paths. There's a section without paths at the crossing, shortly before the holiday complex.
Food and accommodation: bar and restaurant in S. Martino delle Scale. Hotels too in Monreale and Palermo. Accommodation in the L'Abbazia Benedictine monastery on enquiry (rather rustic).

South-west of Palermo, in the hinterland of Monreale, lies the small town of San Martino delle Scale with an old abbey from the 6th century. The Arabians destroyed the monastery and the Normans rebuilt it. Today it's still a Benedictine abbey and the church is also a training workshop for fine art. The 'Academia Abadir' is set up in one of the halls. You will enjoy the most beautiful view of Conca d'Oro and Palermo on this walk.

From the car park go directly up to the picnic area in the **pine grove** and past this you reach a broad path. The cemetery is on the left below. The rocky chain of Serra dell'Occhio is visible and your summit with an observation hut nearby on the right. You gain height round some hairpin bends. After 15 mins. you come to a conspicuous rib of rock which runs down left across the slope. Zigzag up the path below this to a cross path. Go left here and at the next two cross paths. The path then levels out. Straight ahead you reach a knoll. The monastery lies to the left below. Across the olive groves to the right you can see the Villaggio Montano holiday complex. The path here veers up sharply to the right and another descends down to the left. Go along the narrow path to the right crossing the slope. The path ahead is overgrown and gets lost. Keeping at the same height you come to the pine forest which you saw from a distance and you meet a broad path. This joins the tarmac road on a bend which you then follow to the right. After 200m take a sharp right turn onto a narrow road. Ascend this and go right at the turn-off. Go along beside the fence, past an iron gate. The path ascends round a bend and joins a track. Bear right to the **Timpone di Caronìa**. The valley with the cemetery lies below on the left and behind it a rock pyramid with the apt name of Monte Petroso. You also get an uninterrupted view of Conca d'Oro, the golden shell. 'Totally transported as I was, I felt the greatest pleasure. The town facing north, at the foot of high mountains …' If Goethe had seen Palermo from up here on his arrival his 'delight' would have known no bounds. You can feast your eyes on the view to the sea at the Golfo di Castellammare and the Golfo di Carini with Isola delle Fémmine. The view of the Conca d'Oro accompanies you for most of the way on the descent.

Descend the forest road and, going right at two turn-offs, arrive at **Portella Sta. Anna**. Stay on the road and go below the steep slopes of Pizzo Ilici as far as the next right-hand turn-off. You can either take a shortcut here or stay on the forest road which leads you further below, directly to the **pine grove**.

Palermo, embedded in the Conca d'Oro, and the Benedictine monastery in the pine grove.

32 Monte Gallo, 527m

Mondello – in the days when it was a fishermen's village

Fishing harbour – forest entrance – Ex Semaforo – Bauso Rosso – forest entrance – fishing harbour

Location: Mondello.
Starting point: fishing harbour of Mondello. Signs indicating Mondello as you drive out of Palermo as well as on the motorway. Park in the centre.
Walking times: harbour – forest entrance ¾ hr., forest entrance – Ex Semaforo 1¼ hrs., Ex Semaforo – forest entrance ¾ hr., forest entrance – harbour ¾ hr.; total time 3½ hrs.
Ascent: 530m.
Grade: zigzags lead steeply uphill on the second part of the ascent. The paths are obvious, but not marked.
Food and accommodation: good selection of bars, restaurants and hotels in Mondello.

In the 16th century only a *tonnara* (tuna processing plant) with the appropriate tower was given the name of Mondello. Travel writers from the 19th century also gave reports of some fishermen's houses: 'If you want to make a trip into this area you should take your own supplies since the few families living here bake only just enough bread for themselves.' You can see then what became of this small fishing village behind Palermo when you start the walk. From the mooring at the **fishing harbour** go across the Piazza and left past the well. Take the second road on the right and left again when you reach the cross-road. You come to a large car park with a row of villas above and further up, the limestone cliffs of the Monte Gallo massif. Go round the car park and take the little road on the left of it up to the cross-road. From here follow the second broad road (Via Tolomea) to the left and go straight on for about ¼ hr. along a high wall. Before the road goes downhill just before a villa, turn right. The ascent starts here. You reach the **forest entrance** at a green iron gate. Zigzag up along the forest road. Looking back through the pine wood you can see the never-ending ugly building site of the new S. Tomaso Natale housing development. After over 1 hr. the path levels out on a col. The former lighthouse and derelict buildings are visible on the left. Straight ahead there's a view of Monte Pellegrino near Palermo. Leave the path here for a detour to the left and climb the **Ex Semaforo**, the highest point of the walk. From the top you can see over to Capo Zafferano in the east. The solitary Palermitan mountains stand protectively around Conca d'Oro, the Golden Shell. By the first rain in winter the limestone massif of Monte Gallo is transformed into a sea of flowers. Numerous orchids and species of Ophrys and other flowers grow between the rocks.

Back at the turn-off go left, gently ascending to the east. The descent begins on a hilltop, with a beautiful view of Mondello. The path, broad at the start, becomes a mule track and leads to a pond used for extinguishing fires. Pass it on the right and cross the slope of **Bauso Rosso** to the west. Descend left at a turn-off until you reach the forest road and your ascent path. Return along this to the **fishing harbour**.

Mondello with Monte Pellegrino.

33 'Lo Zingaro' nature reserve

Sicily's number one conservation area

Park entrance – Baglio Cosenza – Grotta dell'Uzzo – park entrance

Location: Scopello.
Starting point: south entrance of the park, 100m. From Castellammare on the SS 187 in the direction of Tràpani. From the Scopello exit another 8km, past the small village, to the 'Riserva naturale dello Zingaro'. Large car park.
Walking times: park entrance – Borgo Cosenza 2 hrs., Borgo Cosenza – Grotta dell'Uzzo 1½ hrs., Grotta dell'Uzzo – park entrance 1½ hrs.; total time 5 hrs.
Ascent: 650m.
Grade: easy walk on well-made paths with signs, but long and without shade.
Food and accommodation: guest house in Scopello, *agriturismo* and rooms for rent. Hotels in San Vito Lo Capo and Castellammare.

The nature reserve, Parco Lo Zingaro, the first nature reserve in Sicily, came about through a citizen initiative in 1981 thus preventing the construction of a road between Scopello and S. Vito lo Capo. Today you are able to take a pleasant hike along the improved paths, once used by the shepherds, between the sea and the mountain slopes. The path goes from the **park entrance** past the information hut (where you must register) through a rock tunnel. Further on walk parallel to the coast, past various amenities like picnic areas, the natural history museum and information centre. Paths lead off to idyllic bays where you can swim. You come to the houses of **Zingaro** hamlet in the midst of almond, olive and carob trees. After a 1¼ hrs. walk you reach the turn-off for Sughero and Cosenza. This path ascends to the left for 20 mins. as far as the ruined houses of **Sughero**. The path turns off right next to the upper houses and leads north to the next group of houses, **Baglio Cosenza**. This plateau lies fallow today, but was once heavily cultivated. The park authorities are gradually having the farm restored. After an ascent of ½ hr. you reach the

The European dwarf palm, Palma nana, grows at the side of the path. M. Inici in the background.

highest point of the walk at 500m at a right hand turn-off towards Località Uzzo. The austere Monte Aci and Pizzo Cancela rise up ahead. Descend right, come past a spring and eventually after 40 mins. reach the broad coastal path. Left goes to the north entrance of the park and to S. Vito lo Capo. You go right and 10 mins. later arrive at a park building. Products of the dwarf palm (*Palma nana*) are manufactured here with much flair and old agricultural tools and equipment are on display. Together with the only indigenous palm in Europe, the dwarf palm, you will also find the Manna ash.

Soon after the exhibition centre you come to the **Grotta dell'Uzzo**. Excavations have uncovered relics from the Stone Age. The path ascends again and ¼ hr. after the cave you come past the turn-off to Cosenza.

Walk back from here to the **park entrance** in 1¼ hrs.

34 Monte Monaco, 532m

Viewing balcony above San Vito lo Capo

Villa Sara – col – Monte Monaco

Location: San Vito lo Capo.
Starting point: Villa Sara, 113m. From S. Vito on the ring road towards Parco dello Zingaro. From the sign-posted turn-off left to the Tonnara del Secco drive another 2.2km as far as a cement road on the right.
Walking times: Villa Sara – col 1 hr., col – M. Monaco ½ hr., return 1¼ hrs.; total time 2¾ hrs.
Ascent: 430m.
Grade: the walk is easy and runs along obvious paths. You need to take special care between the quarries in the summit area.
Food and accommodation: good selection in San Vito lo Capo.
Alternative: Pizzo di Sella, 704m. The conspicuous rocky peak on the left of the path is an inviting, but demanding detour for sure-footed hikers. Go above the last farm on the right past the foundations of some old huts, head for the ridge above and along this to the rock formation. Climb over the rocks on the ridge up to the highest point (235m, 1½ hrs.).

On the drive to the starting point and from the walk you can see the Tonnara del Secco by the sea below the steep rocks of M. Monaco. The tuna fishery has recently been restored and is open for visits. Tuna fishing in Sicily has a long tradition. The 'Mattanza', a real battle, is still fought today by all the daring and bold men of the community. However, only in the area of Trápani, in Bonagía and Favignana is it still an important line of business, but with the decline in the fish stock, other *tonnare* have been closed down here as well. If there were 70 of them in the 18th century, you could count them on one hand today.

Go a few metres along the cement road up to the **Villa Sara**. The surfaced road finishes just past the villa. A broad path on the right leads round some bends to the **col** between M. Monaco and P. di Sella. There's a viewing point by the path where you can look down over the coast. Numerous villas, tucked in among green macchia, occupy the beautiful bays. Beyond them to the east you can see wide areas of the coast: the M. Gallo massif, the limestone mountains around Punta Raisi and the gulf of Castellammare. The path leads across a level section past two small farmhouses. Pizzo di Sella rises up above.

Head towards the easily visible peak of M. Monaco along the main path straight on. The abandoned quarries are to be found past a left hand turn-off. It will take a while before grass grows over them. Between the quarries (be careful of the crevices!) you go to a square cistern and past that round a right hand bend to the highest point of **Monte Monaco** (be careful!). Sheer rock faces drop down vertically to the S. Vito plain. This gives a bird's eye view of the fishing port and the gleaming white sandy beaches which invite you to a swim. P. di Sella displays itself in the south-west, with M. Cófano behind and in the distance Erice and the Égadi islands.

Go back down the same path to the road.

View of S. Vito from the summit.

35 Monte Cófano, 659m

The 'casket' high above the sea

Cala Buguto – Monte Cófano – Tonnara di Cófano – Torre San Giovanni – Cala Buguto

Locations: Custonaci and Cornino.
Starting point: Cala Buguto. Follow the signs to Cornino Lido along the stretch to S. Vito lo Capo near Custonaci. Head for M. Cófano along beside the sea. Possible to park at the end of the tarmac road below the housing estate.
Walking times: Cala Buguto – col ¾ hr., summit detour 1½ hr., col – *tonnara* ¾ hr., *tonnara* – Cala Buguto 1¼ hrs.; total time 4¼ hrs.
Ascent: 700m.
Grade: although not an arduous walk, there are a few rocky sections to the summit which makes it a demanding mountain route. The path across the rock slabs is marked red (arrows). At the last rock spur a rope has been put up for safety.
Food and accommodation: bars, restaurant in Custonaci and Cornino. Hotels too in S. Vito lo Capo and Erice.

Cófano (casket) is a captivating mountain with its isolated position and spectacular view. Its surrounding area is today characterised by the mining of marble. Deserted pastures are reminders of former pastoral farming, and the closed-down *tonnara*, of the old tuna fishing tradition.

At **Cala Buguto** head towards the craggy M. Cófano and after the villa district take the third road up to the right. This leads to a marble quarry. After 10 mins., at the end of the estate, the road swings to the right. Keep to the left. Wind up the slope directly below the marble cliffs. Looking back you will see Erice on Erix mountain and also the Égadi islands. The path leads past some large solitary rocks, then becomes a narrow track and zigzags uphill. At a side road on the left you eventually come to the **col**, also called Bivio di Cófano. From here you can see across the Golfo di Cófano to M. Monaco in the distance above S. Vito.

Steep rocks lead up to M. Cófano and there's an huge boulder standing right by the path in front of it. Beyond the boulder a steep well-trodden path leads at first slightly to the west uphill. Then red arrows point to the right into a dihedral cleft. Climb up to a shoulder and there's a safety rope on the upper rock section (I+). Above this you come to the green slopes. It's easier-going from here, but you need to memorise the return to this edge. Walk for a good ½ hr. over rocky, overgrown terrain up to the summit of **Monte Cófano**. The view is stunning.

Return to the col on the same path. Then continue your walk northwards and keeping to the right, begin the descent. The path winds down the slope. The **tonnara** and watch tower come into view. You reach the beach between six foot high grass and meet a road. Go left here. There's a path again at the end of the road which brings you round M. Cófano. Past a small wayside chapel you come to the **Torre S. Giovanni**. Continue along a road beside the sea to reach **Cala Buguto** and the car park across the tarmac.

Evening light on M. Cófano: Cornino and Erice with the Égadi islands.

36 Coste di San Antonino, 625m

An idyllic part of Sicily's interior

San Carlo – Fiume Sósio – Castello Gristía – Portella Rossa – Coste di San Antonino – San Carlo

Locations: S. Carlo, Burgio, Bisacquino.
Starting point: the old railway station at S. Carlo, 248m. From the south the SS 386 via Burgio or from the north via Bisacquino and Chiusa S. as far as the car park.
Walking times: San Carlo – Fiume Sósio ½ hr., F. Sósio – C. Gristía 1 hr., C. Gristía – turn-off to the summit ½ hr., summit ascent 1½ hr., turn-off – S. Carlo 1 hr.; total time 4½ hrs.
Ascent: 523m.
Grade: the crossing of the F. Sósio is more difficult if the water is high. The first part of the ascent is steep. Obvious, but unmarked paths.
Food and accommodation: bars, restaurants in Burgio, Chiusa S. Guest house in Palazzo A.

There are many contrasting surprises in store for you when you visit the area around Fiume Sósio. It has its source at Prizzi and fills a reservoir at Palazzo Adriano. At San Carlo it winds stubbornly round the steep slopes and together with the Fiume Verdura finally flows seawards.

From the former railway station at **San Carlo** head towards the steep rocks along the rail track. Before the big right hand bend take a turning off left, paved at the start, below some house ruins. First the path goes along the side of some bridge pillars, then you turn away from these and walk parallel to the valley, past a house and through a pine forest. Then descend to the right to the **Fiume Sósio** and continue on the broad path left along the bank as far as the crossing. Be careful! Cross the river over to the level ground which you come to through an opening in the fence and you will see a path opposite on the left. Slip under the next fence and go gently uphill along the path, overgrown at the start, round long zigzags.

On a straight section (the return path), ¼ hr. after the river crossing, wind up right across the steep flanks. At a junction take the lower path to a col, go uphill and right at the turn-off to the **Castello Gristía** (remains of foundations). Back at the turn-off continue right. The path descends briefly, then goes up to a ridge. Descend through a eucalyptus wood, through an opening in the fence, onto the now broad path. Go downhill and left at the next

122

turn-off, **Portella Rossa**. On a conspicuous left-hand bend of the forest road where the slope has been reinforced, turn sharp right up a mountain path. On a gentle incline you eventually reach **Coste di San Antonino**, the highest point of the walk with a rewarding view. You can see Chiusa S. and Bisacquino in the north. Monte Trione rises above.

Back at the turn-off go along the track to the right as far as a firebreak. Cross this at the upper edge to the narrow path opposite. Keeping at the same height, past the turn-off for the ascent, descend to the river and **San Carlo** railway station.

The path leads on the right across the flank to the ruins of Castello Gristía.

37 Monte Conca, 437m

A mountain with views and a fascinating 'underworld'

Car park – Monte Conca – Rocche di Tullio – car park

Location: Milena.

Starting point: car park near to the cave of M. Conca, 322m. On the link route Palermo – Agrigento (SS 189) about 27km before Agrigento turn off to Milena/Riserva Naturale M. Conca. After about 4½km there's a car park on the right below an estate (sign: 'Inghittitoio di M. Conca').

Walking times: car park – M. Conca ½ hr., M. Conca – bridge ¾ hr., bridge – Rocche di Tullio ½ hr., Rocche di Tullio – car park 1¼ hrs.; total time 3 hrs.

Ascent: 400m.

Grade: easy walk on marked paths (wooden posts). Sure-footedness is essential on the first part of the descent.

Food and accommodation: bars and restaurants in Milena. Hotels in Agrigento and surrounding area.

NB: the authorities of the nature reserve offer excursions through the unique cave, although for the best part of the trip you need to be able to abseil. Beginners receive some brief training. Register at: Riserva Naturale Monte Conca, Via Pietro Nenni, 4, I-93010 Milena, tel. and fax: 0934/933254.

In the immediate hinterland of Agrigento, near to the popular archaeological site, the nature reserve of Monte Conca stretches over 245 hectares. The conservation area, once rarely visited, was given over to the Italian Alpine Club for development in 1995 by the Sicilian authorities and has many treasures to offer. Large quantities of water over millions of years have resulted in a huge limestone well in the soft rock containing gypsum. M. Conca, located amongst almond groves and three typically sleepy villages, is an inviting place for a varied walk.

Opposite the **car park** an unsurfaced road leads to the north, with views of the pointed castle mound of Sutera. At the turn-off left you pass a country house as you go leisurely downhill to the next turn-off. The right-hand path, overgrown with vegetation, leads down to the cave entrance. Continue straight ahead along the link path between Milena and Campofranco and bear right at the next fork. The path goes uphill and gets lost over the stony ground. Later on cross the slope and ascend round a bend to the right. On a level section, just before the summit, there are some conspicuously large stone blocks. They are the ruins of a Byzantine settlement dating from the 6th century. You arrive at **Monte Conca** along the broad ridge. From here you can enjoy a wonderful panorama: Etna in the east above Milena and the Madonie in the north-east. The villages of Sutera with the conspicuous

The landscape north of Monte Conca.

rocks and Campofranco come into view in the north. The 1600m high Monte Camarata rises up in the west and you can see the Gallo d'Oro river with the ruined bridge below. After heavy rainfall the river is full and the sand bank can become flooded.

The descent route – you need to be sure-footed over the first few metres – goes on the west side. First descend a few paces to the north and keep left at a suitable place. Go downhill across the slope first round narrow, then round long zigzags below the steep slopes of the summit. Reforestation is taking place here. The unclear path continues southwards downhill, some-times round bends. Eventually, behind some large boulders (rather over-grown), it swings down to the right.

After ½ hr. from the summit you meet an old mule track. Bear right here and negotiate a section with large rocks (rock fall), then turn right onto a field path, past the pillars of the bridge, to the **Fiume Gallo d'Oro**. (In the event of high water go back to the mule track and return left round M. Conca, past the cave entrance, to the car park!). Cross the river at a suitable place. After 10 mins. going up to the left you meet a track and bear right. You will see a clump of tall elm trees on the slopes of M. Conca. Fresh water flows out of the cave there. The Gallo d'Oro carries salt water. The steep rock faces of Rocche San Paolino and Rocche di Tullio form a dramatic landscape of gorges. There have recently been eagles and other birds of prey nesting on the rocks.

Keep going along the broad track and continue below beautiful chalky sandstone formations of Rocche di don Michele. A green oasis, **Fontana di Rose**, emerges on the left. The track leads to a group of houses which stand below the col of the two Rocche di Tullio. Shortly before the huts bear left across the fields in front of them and go uphill to the ridge, then descend an obvious path below the rock faces and above the orchards. Through a weird rocky landscape, past a shed in the corner of a rock and through a sheep pen, you eventually find yourself standing above the river and can see the Mezzebbi rocks on the other side. Again you have to cross the river. After crossing it head towards the right-hand side of the slope between P. Paolino and Mezzebbi and go uphill round a big left-hand bend to the col above. The path – now behind the **Mezzebi** – leads past fields in an easterly direction to the road. Go along here to the right and straight on at two other junctions (left goes up to Milena). You come to a water trough and bear left at the turn-off to the **car park**.

Enjoying spring in winter. Monte Conca amidst the fertile fields of Milena.

38 Capo Bianco, 28m

To the archaeological excavations of Heraclea Minoa with swimming gear

Sabbia d'Oro – archaeological excavations – Plátani estuary – Capo Bianco – Sabbia d'Oro

Location: Montallegro.
Starting point: Sabbia d'Oro beach. On the SS 115 Agrigento – Sciacca, past Montallegro, and as far as the sign-posted turn-off 'Cattolica/Eraclea Minoa'. Left here and drive another 3km to a rise. Take the left-hand turn-off down to the beach (signpost 'Rist. Sabbia d'Oro').

Walking times: Sabbia d'Oro – archaeological excavations ½ hr., archaeological excavations – Plátani estuary ¾ hr., Plátani estuary – C. Bianco ½ hr., C. Bianco – Sabbia d'Oro ½ hr., total time 2¼ hrs.
Ascent: 30m.
Grade: the walk goes mainly along obvious, unmarked paths, the second part on the steep cliffs. Be careful of the steep cliffs!
Food and accommodation: bar and restaurant at the starting point. A big choice of hotels in Agrigento and Sciacca.
NB: the swell might prevent you from wading round the rock projection at Capo Bianco, in which case climb over the rocks and return along the path you came on!

You can extend the walk along the lengthy beaches around Capo Bianco as you like. You should not miss visiting the archaeological museum and the archaeological excavations of Heraclea Minoa. The relevant art and travel guides hardly mention this town founded in the 6th century by Selinunt. In the adjoining museum there's a detailed brochure available in several languages. The gleaming white marl cliffs on which it was built gave their name to the cape around which are woven the legends of the flight of Daidal and king Minos' pursuit.

From **Sabbia d'Oro** go back to the tarmac and left up the one way street. Continue up left at the junction, past villas, with the holiday complex visible in the wood on the left below. Go left again at the following junction, walk along beside a wall and down into a hollow. Take an ascending path between fences (olive groves) up to an edge. Bear right along a narrow path at the foundations of the ancient town wall, past the so-called Torre II and afterwards come to the road where you bear left to the archaeological excavations. Across the hills to the right you can see the mountain landscape of Bisaquino. 10 mins. later you are at the entrance to the **archaeological excavations**. Continue from here to the cliffs. The inviting beach extends in

Looking across the white cliffs down to Capo Bianco.

the east as far as Torre Salsa. On the right you pass through two iron gates along a track. After the second, at the edge of the snow-white cliffs (be careful!) you can see Capo Bianco below and beyond to the western part of the beach. Go on ahead and follow the fence on the right for about 10 mins. which runs parallel to the steep cliffs.

A stony path leads down left into the wood. Slightly to the right and then to the south carry on to the beach which you reach at the **Plátani estuary**. Many kinds of heron and numerous other birds visit this estuary. From here go along the beach to the left to **Capo Bianco** and continue to the end of the beach. A high, steep cliff towers up ahead.

If the waves allow it you can wade round this rock projection (see NB!) and return along the beach to **Sabbia d'Or**.

The south-east

The **Hyblaean limestone tableland** probably emerged from the sea in two periods between early Tertiary and Tertiary. The geological relationship of this plateau with North African landscape suggests that the dividing line between the European and African continents is in this region. However complex the speculations are about the geology of the south-eastern corner of Sicily, their structure is clearly evident: the limestone surface rises gradually from sea-level and reaches a height of just under 1000m with **Monte Lauro**. The high plateau itself, seen from a distance, is aptly named 'tableland'. However the valleys, *cave*, deeply cut by rivers which you would never expect from a distance, are its characteristic feature. As you descend into the gorges the high plateau is quickly forgotten. Tall rock faces and towers announce the presence of real mountains: **Monti Iblei**. Climate and vegetation in the third 'valley of the foothills', the so-called Val di Noto, differ greatly from the conditions in the rest of Sicily: hot and dry in summer, mild and green in winter. Nevertheless you can still cope with the heat in summer at the coast as there's always a pleasant breeze blowing off the sea. In the south, at **Capo Passero** and nearby, there still exist some valuable

wetlands which are visited by migratory and marshland birds, amongst others. The rivers and their estuaries are covered in plane trees, willows and the evergreen kermes oaks. The whole area is a sea of blossom from November to May. Another feature of these mountains are the kilometre long dry-stone walls crossing the gently rolling hill country. They separate fields, pastures, orchards and communities. Sometimes they run in double rows in between which they used to drive their herds, to keep them from escaping. Like the Great Wall of China they run up and down over the slopes. This is the cradle of Sicily's several thousand year old culture. Thousands of burial chambers, rock churches and cave

Flower festival in Noto.

dwellings have been skilfully built into the steep rocks of the *cave*. Traces of them date from the 12th century. Before the Hellenistic occupation the original inhabitants of the coast withdrew into the hidden valleys. From Syrakus, the Hyblaean tableland has been systematically reinforced. Enclaves like **Casmene** or **Acréide** were created. In the year 1693 wide areas of eastern Sicily were struck by a devastating earthquake. **Noto** was completely destroyed and rebuilt in baroque style. Other towns took over the style and each one, no matter how small, still has elements of Sicilian baroque today. Keeping this in mind as you take a round trip, you should visit the towns of **Ferla**, **Palazzolo Acréide** and **Militello** as well as Noto. The cultural high point of a trip into the south-east of Sicily is **Syrakus**. The archaeological museum, the Greek theatre, the Latomie and the cathedral, as well as the old town with its narrow streets, small shops and the food market are all worth a visit. A journey through the festivals of southern Sicily is like walking through the waves of history of this island. The most colourful festivities take place in Palazzolo Acréide at the end of June in honour of Saint Paul. Multi-coloured paper strips are shot into the air which then rain down over the processions. The feast of Saint Sebastian in **Mellile** between Sortino and Augusta becomes a genuine seeking for absolution. Streams of pilgrims from every Hyblaean village make their way to the festival – bare-foot!

131

39 Vendicari nature reserve

A nature reserve for the protection of turtles

Park entrance – Pantano Piccolo – Calamosche

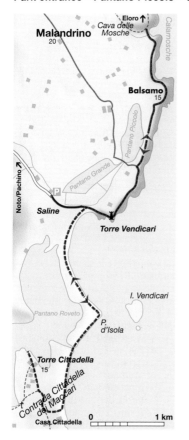

Location: Noto.

Starting point: south entrance to the reserve. From Syrakus or Noto in the direction of Noto Marina. Shortly before, take the turn-off to Pachino and drive 8km as far as the Riserva Naturale Vendicari (sign-posted) and 1km further on to the car park.

Walking times: park entrance – Pantano Piccolo ½ hr., Pantano Piccolo – Calamosche ½ hr., return 1 hr.; total time about 2 hrs.

Ascent: 10m.

Grade: easy walk on obvious paths, waymarkers. No shade!

Food and accommodation: large choice of hotels in Noto Marina. *Agriturismo* right by Vendicari.

Alternative: it's well worth walking along the beach southwards to the so-called Torre Cittadella in order (hopefully) to do some bird-watching. First walk along the beach, then keeping right, past the Pantano Roveto, to the 'Cittadella' (marked). You can still make out the church of a Byzantine settlement (6th century). There and back in 1½ hrs.

Vendicari, a conservation area since 1989, offers an ideal habitat for numerous species of birds. This biotope of macchia scrub and wetlands is also used as a stopping-off point by migratory birds on their journey between Europe and Africa. Turtles have been coming here recently sometimes. Environmentalists hope that this endangered species will frequent the coast of Vendicari as their breeding ground. This is the reason for there being a ban on swimming throughout the nature reserve so that the giant turtles might be protected!

From the information hut at the **park entrance** (register here) a broad path leads through the salt-pan at the **Pantano Grande** to the sea. The island of Vendicari lies off the coast. The path leads left beyond the *tonnara* to a rock jutting out into the sea. The tall chimney of the *tonnara* and the **tower of Vendicari** would tell us about past centuries if they could. The flat promontory with its 'pools' is evidence of a century old culinary tradition: even the Greeks used to process tuna fish here. To the left, past various buildings and along a dry-stone wall you come to the **Pantano Piccolo** after ½ hr. On the other side of the lake you can see the baroque town of Noto and the Hyblaean plateau. Descend to the right, past the 'small lake' and after 20 mins. continue along a bordered by-path. Numerous macchia plants, beaten into dwarf shapes by the west wind, and many aromatic herbs enhance this short walk. Eventually after just under 1 hr. you come to the **Calamosche** on the right. Turtles breed close to the beach here in May/June. The path opposite leads across the Fiume Tellaro and on to the archaeological excavations of the ancient town of Eloro (8 BC). Crossing the Tellaro estuary depends on the water level and is sometimes difficult, even impossible, but you can also reach ancient Eloro by going over the road. Descend the steps to the right down to the sandy bay for an enjoyable rest before returning to the **park entrance**.

Views of the Hyblaean mountains and Noto Marina on the walk.

40 Cava Grande del Cassíbile

At the mountainous edge of the Hyblaean plateau

Belvedere – valley floor – mountain path – 'Laghetti' – Belvedere

Location: Ávola.
Starting point: Belvedere, 480m. From Syrakus via Ávola and Ávola Antica and on the SP 4 past new villas. Go right at the turn-off to the car park at 'Cava Grande'.
Walking times: car park – valley floor 1 hr., start of the valley floor – rock spur 1¼ hrs., rock spur – 'Laghetti' ¾ hr., 'Laghetti' – Belvedere ¾ hr.; total time 3¾ hrs.

Ascent: 600m.
Grade: sure-footedness, fitness and sometimes a good sense of direction are essential. Those sensitive to the heat should not undertake this walk on hot days.
Food and accommodation: bar/*trattoria* at the 'Belvedere'. Rooms for rent in Ávola. Hotels in Lido di Noto.

The mountain path through the 'Grand Canyon' of Sicily leads across dizzy-making precipices, through bizarre ravines shaped by the processes of air and water and past stunning views. You can also spot the nesting places of numerous species of birds in the steep cliffs. In these steep rock faces archaeologists have discovered burial chambers, caves hollowed out by human hand, even whole village complexes which settlers, brigands, shepherds and others have utilised since the time of the Sicanians, from 11 BC to the present day.

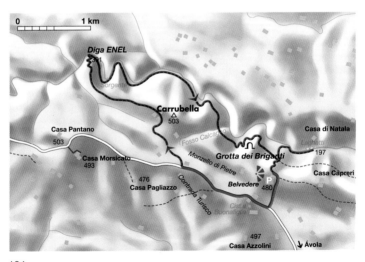

134

From the car park you can see into the last part of the gorge.

From the **Belvedere** you look down into the wild and romantic gorge and to the 'Laghetti', small lakes on the last part of the walk. Syrakus and Rossolini are also visible in the distance. Go back along the road to the turn-off and right along the SP 4. Keep right again at the next fork. A good 5 mins. after the fork bear right at some ruins of houses along the unsurfaced road ('Via Madonna di Lourdes'). The road goes past various villas to a large water container and ends at a farm. Go left and immediately right after the house.

The path ascends over rocky ground and leads through a gate across pasture land past an assortment of buildings. Behind a garage go left and start the descent down some steps into the **Fiume Cassíbile** valley. On the left can be seen the upper reaches of the valley around which there's dense jungle-like undergrowth. 10 mins. later you reach the bottom of the valley and the Italian hydro-electric plant (ENEL). The path leads most of the time along a rock aqueduct which goes at a height of about 300m towards Ávola. At a junction bear right. The path runs parallel to the river, shaded by holm oaks. There are some enormous plane trees in the riverbed.

Be careful: ¼ hr. after the junction you reach a difficult to see, but important turn-off close to the water, which leads up right below large holm oak trees, but first it's well worth taking a leisurely descent past a spring to the river. The water flows between towering cliffs through gullies into pools. A unique biotope has evolved here in the middle of an 'amphitheatre'.

Go back to the spring and then exactly 50 paces back along the path you came on. Now you can see the ascent on the left. This well-made path in the limestone rock goes right round the much-visited 'amphitheatre'. ¼ hr. after the start of the ascent up the rocky path over some steps you come to a junction. A path comes up from the left which continues broadly uphill ahead. You must avoid this!

Carry on at the same height and cross the slope on the less obvious path, at times through dense undergrowth. Keep straight on at another turn-off along the narrow path. The river meanders through a dramatic landscape and you catch sight of the aqueduct ahead on the rock spur. Grotta dei Briganti is above. On the way there you see steep towering cliff faces into which have been hewn burial chambers. You come across some wet rocks (be careful!) and find a memorial plaque out of marble at a cave, hollowed-out by human hand. After crossing the slope for another 15 mins. with dramatic views, the valley suddenly broadens out at the **rock spur** and you can see the sea, the car park up on the right and the path ahead to the 'Laghetti'. You reach a junction 10 mins. later on.

Before you ascend to the car park go downhill to the pools. It's important to find the exact way down. Stay on the main path and do not take any short-cuts! Eventually you reach the river bank down some rock steps and go above it to the pools. Depending on the water level it's pleasant wading across and taking a refreshing swim. Climb back up the same path to the junction and continue to wind uphill to the **Belvedere**.

The water of Cassíbile has created numerous biotopes.

41 Monte Erbesso, 821m

At the Anapo springs

Casa Portella – Fiume Anapo – Casa Cantone – Monte Erbesso/ Casmene – Casa Portella

Locations: Buscemi, Buccheri or Giarratana.

Starting point: eucalyptus grove below the excavations of Casmene, 781m (Casa Portella). On the SS 124 from Syrakus via Palazzolo and Buscemi. Go left just before Buccheri and 9km in the direction of Giarratana as far as a tarmac left-hand turn-off (just before a farm house and a bend in the road). Continue another 800m to the car park (sign-posted 'Casmenai').

Walking times: Casa Portella – Fiume Anapo ¾ hr., Fiume Anapo – rail track 1 hr., rail track – M. Erbesso ¾ hr., M. Erbesso – Casa Portella ½ hr.; total time

3 hrs.

Ascent: 300m.

Grade: easy walk, but only partly marked (red and white). First without paths in places, but no route finding problems. For most of the way without shade.

Food and accommodation: bars, *trattoria*, rooms for rent in Buscemi. Hotels in Buccheri as well.

NB: the community of Buscemi offers guided walks in the surrounding area. In the village old houses have been converted into museums, where there's a display of traditions and craftwork. Tel: 0931878273.

A volcanic hill rises up above the source area of the Anapo and was for over thousands of years a strategically advantageous spot with its broad plateau. The fortified town of Casmene (Casmenai) lay on this plateau,

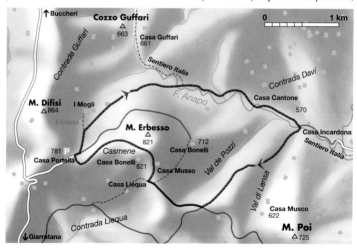

Actually we only wanted to ask the way ... Palazzolo Acréide in the background.

between Acréide, today Palazzolo, and Camarina, south-west of Ragusa. The Greek Syracusans founded the town in the 7th century BC. With the decline of Syrakus, 212 BC, the Casmenians emigrated to Giarratana. At present archaeologists are uncovering what there is left of the glittering era of the fortification. But the fertile hill country of the Hyblaeans is more fascinating than the excavations.

From the car park, **Casa Portella**, go in the direction of the traffic along a broad path past the entrance to the excavations (the return path). After a few paces descend a narrow path to the left. Past a water trough head for the ruins of some houses on the left. The former estate fell victim to the violent earthquake which destroyed the whole of eastern Sicily in 1693. On the right of the ruins go straight on, past another water trough. M. Lauro, the highest point of Monte Iblei covered in aerials and the pine forest of Buccheri come

139

Star anemones (Anemone hortensis).

into view on the left. The springs of Anapo are to be found below them, by the houses of Guffari. Ahead on the right you can see Buscemi. The path goes downhill and gets lost in the pasture area. Head for an easily visible stone wall and before you reach the bottom of the valley, go right. Stay on the open ground above, parallel to the valley. Where the dry-stone wall is interrupted by a tall rock go downhill to the **Fiume Anapo**. Between wall and stream bed you reach a pond, go left over the stream and above the pond meet the red and white waymarkers of the 'Sentiero Italia' which goes from Buccheri to Palazzolo. Now go on the left of the dry-stone wall, which is replaced by a fence later on, out of the valley. Clamber over the third wooden ladder to the right. Opposite, right by the stream on the left, you come to **Casa Cantone** in Contrada Daví. Carry on past the huts to a clump of tall poplars. Afterwards, 15 mins. from Casa Cantone, keep on the 'Sentiero Italia' and cross over the stream a few times. At one point you also climb over a chain to the right. You can see Buscemi on the left, Palazzolo ahead and M. Erbesso behind. You come to a broad path shortly afterwards on which you turn right (on the left there's a works yard). The path gets narrow again and leads into the bend of a road. Leave the 'Sentiero Italia' here and go across the stream to the right (straight on brings you to the tarmac road to Buscemi). Now begins the ascent. Anapotal lies to the right. Later you come along a ridge, between Val di Lensa and Val de Pozzi, past some more ruins of houses. After about 35 mins. uphill the path joins the old rail track where the Palazzolo train to the south used to run. At this multi-junction go up along the track furthest to the right towards M. Erbesso. 30 mins. after the turn-off you come to Casa Musso. Keep to the left just before-hand to reach the high plateau of **Casmene** on **M. Erbesso**. Above in the north you can see M. Lauro again and in the west a little house which you head towards.

Keep to the left, cross the plateau past some excavations and descend to a broad path which, to the right, brings you back to the car park at **Casa Portella**.

At Casa Musso: hill country and pasture-land as far as the eye can see.

42 Pantálica

Dwelling places, churches and tombs in the rock

North necropolis – Fiume Anapo – Oratorio di S. Micidiario – Belvedere (south necropolis) – Anaktoron – north necropolis

Location: Sortino.

Starting point: car park at the north necropolis, 330m. From Sortino follow the signs to Pantálica/Valle Calcinara for about 6km to the car park at the end of the tarmac road.

Walking times: north necropolis – Anapo 20 mins., Anapo – Belvedere 1 hr., Belvedere – Anaktoron ¾ hr., Anaktoron – north necropolis ¾ hr.; total time 2 hrs. 50 mins.

Ascent: 400m.

Grade: easy walk, mainly on obvious paths. Two river crossings on stepping stones.

Food and accommodation: bars, pizzeria, rooms for rent in Sortino, hotels in Syrakus and Palazzolo.

NB: Vincenzo Briganti from Sortino, 'inhabitant of Pantálica' by profession and extremely helpful, offers guided walks, tel: 0931952489 and 3398909137 (mobile).

The deep clefts and steep cliffs of the limestone gorges in the Hyblaean mountains are natural fortresses and ideal hiding places. People have found refuge here in all periods of history. They had built houses, places of prayer and tombs since the 13th century BC. Over 5000 tombs have been discovered in this, the largest necropolis of classical antiquity.

From the car park at the **north necropolis** go a few metres back along the tarmac road and just after an iron gate you find a ladder over a fence which you climb over. Descend across pastures, past almond and carob trees. Wind downhill at a house ruin on the right to the **Fiume Anapo**.

After crossing the river go a few more paces until you meet a broad path along which you continue to the right. An aqueduct runs along the steep rock wall on the right which, in ancient times, once carried the water of the Calcinara river as far as Syrakus. Unusually, the holes hewn into the rocks here are not burial chambers, but air holes for the water conduit. Walk for

¼ hr. up and down in between and over the rocks until you reach the former rail track next to a tunnel, the old stretch of railway between Syrakus and Ragusa. On the right you come across a bridge to a tunnel and just under 10 mins. after that, to the turn-off 'Percorsi particolari D'. Leave the road here to the right and begin the ascent on a well-made path.

Partly over rocky ground, partly up some stone steps, you pass burial chambers and go straight on to a rock face with a row of rock dwellings and tombs. Keep to the left here and continue going uphill wherever the path divides. There's a yellow sign for **'Belvedere Necropoli Sud'**. The path levels out here and after a ½ hr. ascent it goes gradually downhill again. Across the Anapo valley you can see the green covered rock slopes and side valleys.

At the next left-hand turn-off stay on the main path crossing the slope. 5 mins. later you reach a large complex of dwelling places and tombs, but above all, the **Oratorio di S. Micidiario**, a Byzantine rock church. At the Oratorio continue to walk along the main path. There are hundreds of burial chambers in the surrounding rock slopes. Through a gate you come to a

A place for a rest by the Fiume Anapo.

tarmac road. Just before it, go right along an ascending path and come to another gate. Beyond that go first right, then left, gently uphill as far as a gap in the fence. Through the gap you come onto a plateau. Go straight on along some well-trodden paths and then descend into a hollow to the **Anaktoron** you saw from above. Archaeologists have discovered between the megalithic walls traces of a foundry, amongst other things. To the north you can see the little town of Sortino, with Etna rising up behind. The Valle Calcinara lies below Sortino.

Descend left along an unsurfaced road to the tarmac road. Go right along this to the end, then continue along a broad path. Again, walk on a path cut into the stone which leads through a rocky landscape down to the river. After crossing the river go uphill again on the other bank. This especially delightful part of the walk is called **'Nekropoli Nord'**. Numerous burial chambers show the importance of these prehistoric necropolises.

By the end of the walk you have gone all the way round the Calcinara valley. During the last part keep right through a gap in the wall and eventually return to the starting point.

A sea of flowers on the plateau of Pantálica.

Across the north necropolis near Sortino.

Lipari or Aeolian islands

The Aeolian islands lie off the north coast of Sicily, right along the route of volcanoes between Vesuvius and Etna. They are fiery and eerie, nevertheless appealing and not without an air of Mediterranean charm, which can cause you to be misled about the dangers within. Each one is evidence of a turbulent past. Many of them are still stirring today. The fact that their future will not be exactly peaceful is keeping the scientists busy. In the Tyrrhenian sea, south of Naples and north of the Aeolians, active volcanoes of considerable dimensions and liveliness exist below sea level. If there had been an addition to the family of the seven sisters in the Lipari archipelago, they would have been ready with Christian names: Marsili, for example, is the name of a restless volcano, just under 1km below sea level. An eruption, however, would not be without its consequences. Sea quakes and tidal waves could devastate the coasts of southern Italy and the Aeolian islands. Despite the relatively recent origin of the islands, that would be nothing new. The submarine volcanic ruins show an age of more than two million years. So, like the peaks of high volcanoes rising up out of the sea today, they are about 350,000 years young. Hikes in the region of the Aeolian islands are at a level above that of the ordinary 'Mediterranean island hopping' and become an exciting exploration of a 'laboratory made of magma': experiencing the wild sulphur pools, fumaroles and minerals, basalt, pumice and obsidian and getting to know the enormous volcanic apparatus of the archipelago.

Strómboli is the most active volcano and very famous. It lies in the eastern corner of the archipelago and nearer to Calabria. From a distance you can see the whole of the cone and understand the origin of its name from the Greek Strongyle, 'the rounded island'. It has never once since its evolution relinquished its constant activity. If you approach it from the east, you will experience it – today as in classical antiquity – like a lighthouse in the open sea. Its north-west flank, Sciara del Fuoco, is the slide for the volcanic detritus which spews out of the crater. The 900m long trail of fire sinks into the sea at least as steeply and as deeply. Scientists and tourists have been visiting the island for centuries and the volcano is the main attraction for everyone, Strombolians, too, who have totally commercialised it. They see a greater catastrophe in the 'inactivity' of the volcano.

Panarea has cooled extensively, and only a few fumaroles bubble away in the north of the island. The island is known for its rich and famous visitors and its accommodation to a very high standard. Those who had once landed in Panarea with a rucksack, would have been branded automatically as 'flower people looking for a thousand-star accommodation' and were not welcome. This, the smallest of the Aeolians, is separated from the other islands below sea level by immense gorges, but forms an independent volcano together with the rocky outlying islands nearby, Basiluzzo, Lisca Bianca, Nera, le Formiche etc.

Lipari lies further south with hot springs and fumaroles. It is the largest island and in the centre of this group. To the north of Lipari are to be found the pumice deposits of Monte Pilato and Monte Chirica. Before their industrial use in the 19th century, pumice was quarried with pick and axe and taken away on the backs of animals and people. Quarrying used to promote slavery in classical antiquity and in modern times, 'Liparose' is a disease of the lungs which workers in the quarries were still suffering from 20 years ago. Pumice is used in the construction and paper industries, just as it is for stone-washed jeans. The heavy obsidian, the black gold of antiquity, is on the other hand no longer in demand.

The sulphur fumes on the powder keg of **Vulcano** is considerably more intensive than on Lipari. Vulcanello, which emerged from the sea between Vesuvius and Etna, was the youngest volcano in 183 BC. This resulted in a devastating loss of fish, amongst other things, which was reported by Plinius the Elder. In the 6th century lava flows joined Vulcano and Vulcanello together. Health conscious Italians and foreign tourists wallow in the fumaroles on the isthmus near the beach. About a litre of 'biologically pure' mud exudes every minute and has an average temperature of 34 °C. The

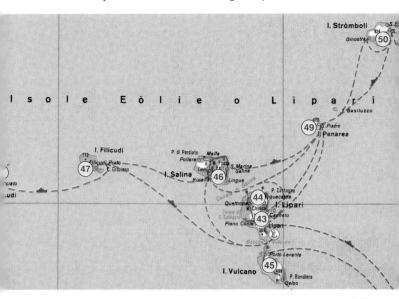

last big eruption was a long time ago. In 1889 the upper part of the mountain was blasted into the air. With it went more than the possessions of the Scot called Stevenson who was extracting alum and sulhur. A bigger explosion of the Gran Cratere could cover Lipari with ejected material or worse still, blast it into the air. A smaller one would pretty well cover the region in dust.

The volcanoes on **Salina** are now extinguished and the island is getting greener. Since 1867 Salina has been self-sufficient and independent from the Lipari administration and is becoming known as 'the stubborn island'. It has two perfect cones, no longer active, and the Greeks called it Didyme, 'the double island'. Its name has been Salina since Roman times because of the lagoon near Lingua where salt was extracted. The island is a producer of capers and Malmsey wine and is therefore also called 'the green island'. The inhabitants make their living from agriculture and forestry. Tourism is gradually on the up: the new 'Museo Etno-Antropologico' in the Lingua area is connected to this.

Filicudi, the 'island without shade', is how those would describe it who climb Fossa Felci in the summer months. Felci (ferns) also lent their name to the island in ancient times: Phenicusa, the 'island abundant with ferns'. The steep coasts are ideal for diving, especially in the west where the cliffs rise out of the water in bizarre shapes. But the main attraction of the island is, and remains, the archaeological excavations of Capo Graziano. In the 17th century BC on **Alicudi** there was a Bronze Age settlement which was excavated by archaeologists at Rocca Palumba. Since then settlers have come and gone. However the island was uninhabited between the 14th and the 17th centuries. The tree heathers remained and have thrived for as long as anyone can remember lending their Greek name to the island: Ericusa.

The islands do not only have an exciting geological history. From the Stone Age through classical antiquity and the Middle Ages right up to the present day they have attracted people and stolen their hearts. Obsidian, the 'black gold', played an enormous role in the development of the islands and brought not only the merchant fleet to the western Mediterranean. The god Aiolos and his retinue occupied the islands on their flight fom Greece. The meeting of Odysseus with the ruler of the winds occupies an important chapter in Homer's tale. Still today the Italians use the legendary name of that time: Aeolian islands. The Ausonian dynasty from southern Italy banished this island myth in 1200 BC. Liparus, their king, gave the archipelago its second name.

The latest occupation of this group of islands worldwide has been by poets, scientists, film makers and tourist managers. Since then the island has been called the 'seven beauties'. You can travel there by ferry and hydrofoil from the mainland and from Sicily. A huge choice of round-island boat trips makes it possible to appreciate them from the sea. In bays and thermal springs the visitor can take a cure and day dream. Lipari cuisine is influenced by the north (mainland) and the south (Sicily) – varied and imaginative. Newly developed fish farms are trying to cope with the enormous demand in high season. Malmsey wine and capers from the Lipari islands enrich expensive menus internationally. And the colourful Mediterranean flora attracts hikers to the islands from all over the world – or is it just the explosive nature of its environment?

A sight for the Gods: view from Vulcano across Vulcanello to Lipari.

43 Lipari: Monte Guardia, 369m

The watch tower of Lipari

Capistello – Punta della Crapazza – San Salvatore – Monte Guardia – col on Monte Giardina – Marina Corta

Location: Lipari.

Starting point: Capistello bus stop, 130m. The office of ORSO, local buses, tel: 0909/811262, are to be found at the northern end of Corso near Marina Lunga. The buses travel in all directions from opposite the office. The 'Linea Bianca' goes through the town and to Capistello.

Walking times: Capistello – S. Salvatore ¾ hr., S. Salvatore – M. Guardia 1 hr., M. Guardia – S. Bartolo al Monte 1 hr., S. Bartolo – Marina Corta ½ hr., total time 3¼ hrs.

Ascent: 269m, 399m in descent.

Grade: the easy path runs along a mixture of roads, broad paths, field paths and well-trodden paths. The detour to the summit is rather steep. If you decide to leave it out, there's also an impressive view from the walk round the mountain.

Food and accommodation: large selection. Information: Azienda Autonoma di Soggiorno e Turismso, Corso Vittorio Emmanuele, 202, tel: 0909880095, fax 0909811190, e-mail: aasteolie@netnet.it, http:// www.netnet.it/aasteollie.

NB: Azienda Agrituristica 'Tivoli', Via Quartana, 8, Lipari/Quattropani, tel. and fax 0909886031, open all year round. The Maria Cannistra family also rents out apartments.

Cooperativa 'Il Sentiero', Via Aria Morta, Lipari/Quattropani (ME), tel: 3384793064 (mobile), fax 0909886614, e-mail: sentiero@netnet.it. The members of the co-operative on Lipari and Vulcano support alternative tourism and offer, amongst other things, guided walks.

The Liparis were not safe from attack right into the 18th century and only left the castle as their safety gradually returned. There was once a sentry on the summit of Monte Guardia and not without reason: the whole of the Aeolian archipelago can be seen from here. The views of Vulcano and the isthmus, Canale delle Bocche, as well as of the town and fortified mountain of Lipari are the highlights of this walk.

From **Capistello** go parallel to the road, on the left below it, downhill along a narrow cement roadway and continue straight ahead at the left-hand turn-off. Then on the ascent you come past a domed church and the last holiday houses of Capparo. After that it turns into a surfaced path. With one of the most beautiful views of the island of Vulcano and the Faraglioni go above Punta della Crapazza sharply round to the right, then continue uphill on the left of a dry-stone wall. The outline of Sicily is visible. In clear visibility

On the way to M. Guardia with views down onto the Faraglioni. Vulcano in the background.

The descent with views of Lipari. Monterosa in the background, Panarea and Strómboli on the horizon.

you can see the high mountains of the Madonie and Nebrodie, and Etna too, of course. Come past the villa belonging to the director Sinopoli and you can see Monte Guardia ahead and the volcanological observatory below it. Along a cement path you reach the tarmac road again which leads left to the observatory.

Descend right, go left at a traffic island and at a narrow road, past various villas, you reach the little church of **San Salvatore** dating from the 17th century. At the end of the narrow road you can see across a steep valley to Lipari. Continue left parallel to the valley. The path narrows, goes through tall rushes and up to a col with views left to a gully down to the sea. Then it levels out for 5 mins., turns to the right and heads for M. Guardia. Begin the ascent from a rounded hilltop, before the path descends. The path winds up at first and then the slope gets steeper and you go uphill on a narrow track. On the left of an easily visible rock projection you eventually come onto some level ground and go right to the pre-summit. From here the observatory with the backdrop of Vulcano island appears like a Renaissance palace. **Monte Guardia** lies a few paces to the left. You can see across Lipari and Monterosa over to Panarea and Strómboli. All the islands in one view! M. Guardia does credit to its name.

Go back down the same way to the main path where you turn right. On the left of a hollow with some vines leave the track which goes downhill and go straight on to the col at M. Giardina. Descend left along the surfaced road with views of Lipari and a breathtaking panorama and go past wonderful villas with their typical terraces. The road ends at the turning point for buses below the chapel of **S. Bartolo al Monte**. Go right here along a narrow street steeply downhill. Past orchards the now tarmac road joins a broader road along which you go to the right. This eventually ends at some metal railings. At the right-hand corner go down some steps and left up the first little street. When you arrive at the through-road continue right until, at a left-hand bend, you reach the start of the Corso V. Emmanuele.

Descend right and through the narrow streets you come to the small port, **Marina Corta**.

Typical scene in the old town of Lipari.

44 Lipari: Monte Chirica, 602m

To the highest mountain of the largest island

Quattropani – Piano alta Pecora – Monte Chirica – Fossa Castagna – Fossa delle Rocche Rosse – Acquacalda

Locations: Quattropani, Acquacalda.
Starting point: bus stop 'Bivio Chiesa Vecchia' in Quattropani, 360m. From Lipari with the URSO bus. The office of URSO, local buses, is at Marina Lunga, tel: 0909811262. The buses go in all directions from opposite the office.
Walking times: Quattropani – alta Pecora 1¼ hrs., alta Pecora – M. Chirica ¾ hr., M. Chirica – Rocche Rosse 1¼ hrs., Rocce Rosse – Acquacalda 1 hr.; total time

4¼ hrs.
Ascent: 300m, 650m in descent.
Grade: small variation in height. Nevertheless, give yourself plenty of time. The walk is not marked. A good sense of direction is essential, especially on the first part of the descent.
Food and accommodation: see Walk 43.
NB: see Walk 43.
Reminder: bus service from Acquacalda to Lipari.

Descent from M. Chirica to the col on gleaming white pumice stone.

Monte Chirica is the highest mountain on Lipari island. The descent of the walk described here goes through veins of obsidian and past pumice deposits. Both materials attracted settlers here in ancient times. The two volcanic rocks are closely related, but differ in structure: pumice evolves through the heavy build up of froth of the magma and the sudden release of pressure, obsidian through quick solidification under high pressure. Pumice is still quarried today under the direction of the Pomax firm. Then a blessing and a curse as it is now.

From the bus stop in **Quattropani** (towards Acquacalda) go right (sign 'Santuario Chiesa Vecchia') and up along the parallel road in the direction of the traffic which descends again from the rounded hill-top. Leave it on the bend to the right along a surfaced road and go up as far as the high-ground. After a few paces downhill take the second path ascending to the right. This path is fairly broad and continues, past a turn-off on the right, steeply uphill. It is densely overgrown in the upper section. It leads to a big stone house and joins a track. Go right and then at each of the following turn-offs, straight on. Meanwhile Monte Sant'Angelo emerges ahead and below you the houses of Quattropani. The islands Salina, Alicudi and Filicudi come into view and head towards M. Chirica on the left in front.

The unsurfaced road turns into a tarmac road and briefly goes downhill to a cross-road. Go up left here and at a villa in a pine grove the road swings left and the tarmac ends again. Along the unsurfaced road now continuing on the level, you come to **Piano alta Pecora** with a little pine wood. Again go straight past all the turn-offs to the end of the road and continue on a narrow path which is furrowed with rain channels and gets more and more steep and narrow. Dense vegetation throws a trellis across the path which goes up in a clockwise direction to the summit. Go right at a turn-off (the descent is to the left) to the aerial covered **M. Chirica**. As if on a turn-table you can see all the Aeolians and beyond Vulcano, even Sicily.

After a rest go back to the turn-off and begin the descent straight ahead. The path swings along a ridge to the right and goes downhill. On the left you can see into the **Fossa Castagna**, a large basin, where the path continues. The little church of Lami, Madonna del Rosario, stands prominently on the slopes of M. Pilato. Descend over gleaming white pumice stone to a col and climb up the opposite side again. The broad path levels out and leads straight along a ridge towards M. S. Angelo. Past derelict huts you come to a junction and descend left. Through dense vegetation and across rain gullies go downhill, in places quite steeply, until you meet a broad path at the Fossa Castagna. Go left here and walk leisurely downhill.

Later on you come to two unsurfaced roads where you turn left each time. Now go straight on for about 15 mins. and steeply up into the wood at a right-hand turn-off. On top of the knoll you find a three-way junction: right goes to M. Pilato and a path ascends to the left. Take the middle path to a col. Be careful! Go 100 paces downhill to a broad left hand turn-off. Descend another 100 paces round a right-hand bend and before the next turn-off climb up left along a path hidden in the undergrowth. From now on keep going straight on and the path becomes more obvious.

Descend between strawberry trees which, in the autumn, bear plump-round fruit and blossom at the same time. With Strómboli and Panarea always in your sights, the path descends **Rocche Rosse** (red rock) under which there are deposits of obsidian. To the right and later to the left, you come across steep white pumice stone slopes, smoothly polished like glacial faces. The path curves down to a roadway which you descend to the left. At a turn-off left, then down some steps to the right, you reach the first houses and meet the tarmac road (it goes right via Canneto to Lipari).

Turn left and using steps as a shortcut you come to the old loading point in **Acquacalda**. The bus stop for Lipari is just in front.

On the descent. The path goes through the Valle Castagna at the foot of M. Pilato. Panarea and Strómboli in the background.

45 Vulcano: Gran Cratere, 391m

Health resort on top of a powder keg

Port – crater rim – walk round Gran Cratere – port

Location: Porto di Levante.
Starting point: port.
Walking times: port – crater rim 1 hr., walk round Gran Cratere ¾ hr., descent to the port ¾ hr.; total time 2½ hrs.
Ascent: 391m.
Grade: easy walk. Be careful of the deep gullies as you cross the slope.
Food and accommodation: big selection. For information see Walk 43.
NB: from the port to the right, beyond the alum rocks, you reach the Sorgenti Termali. At a small cost you can take a mud bath in the mud pools (but do not stay in them longer than 20 mins!).
Alternative: from the mud pools go left along the coast across the isthmus and at a hotel you come to the road. Go right here, left at the junction and between the houses, then right along an unsurfaced road to the Valle dei Mostri. Bizarre shapes of solidified lava stand on ash. The Faraglioni rocks and the island of Lipari are near at hand.
Return the same way or along the road. The walk takes about 2 hrs.

Keep away from the sulphur fumes coming from the numerous cracks at the large crater which reach a temperature of up to 200 °C. If these fumes get any hotter or the pressure gets any greater, then there's cause for alarm. The inhabitants are sitting on a powder keg. A wonderful festival takes place every year after the tourist season. When visitors have left there's an evacuation practice and with it much celebration. Vulcano is like Vesuvius: explosive, unfathomable, inactive at present!

From the **port** follow the one-way street on the left towards Piano. Past the supermarket, just before the telephone aerials, leave the street on the left and begin the ascent. In between tall gorse bushes you gain height round some bends and cross the slope of red clay, cut by rainwater runnels. The view is enhanced with each step. You can see all the islands, especially

Lipari. Just before the crater go right up along a narrow path to reach the **crater rim**. The sulphur vents are on the left which you will come past on the return. Go right round the **Gran Cratere** and climb up to its highest point. From the summit you can look over to M. Aria in the east, at 500m the highest elevation on the island. The forest above Piano is on the right of it, Sicily with Etna beyond and you can see all the other islands at one go. From the summit zigzag down quite steeply to the **sulphur pools**. Sulphur crystals, ranging in colour from white to dark yellow, have formed around the steam vents (please do not break them off!). The hot steam requires care at all times. If the wind is unfavourable or the humidity is high you might get caught in an unpleasant cloud of sulphur. The sulphur smell lingers for days after a visit to Vulcano. In classical antiquity sailors recognised the island just from the sulphur.

Walk along the crater rim to the measuring equipment and to the right return to the **port**.

Hot steam emitting from fumaroles at the rim of the crater.

46 Salina: Monte Fossa delle Felci, 962m

Island of superlatives: the greenest of the Aeolians with the highest summit

Santa Marina – Vallone del Castagno – Monte Fossa delle Felci – Santuario Madonna del Terzito

Location: S. Marina Salina.
Starting point: S. Marina port.
Walking times: S. Marina – Vallone Castagno 1 hr., V. Castagno – M. Fossa 2 hrs., M. Fossa – Santuario Terzito 1½ hrs.; total time 4½ hrs.
Ascent: 970m, 680m in descent.
Grade: the walk is marked with wooden boards, the paths are obvious, but mainly steep.

Food and accommodation: good selection in S. Marina, Malfa and Rinella. For information see Walk 43.
Tip: for the return journey make a note of the departure times of the buses from Valdichiesa on the time-table at the ferry office in S. Marina.

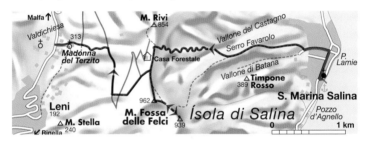

At 962m, Salina is the highest island in the archipelago. There is frequently a cloud cap over the twin volcanoes and the region is also covered in dense woodland. The zones of vegetation are so varied that when you are up in the magnificent wood, you could almost forget you are on one of the Lipari islands.

From the port walk on the right as far as the Piazza (church) in **S. Marina** (ferry offices). Take the road up left before the church (Via Colombo) and go immediately right past various shops, as far as a junction and then left. The road goes uphill past orchards of fruit trees and caper plants. Cross over the main road and after a short while you find a sign which indicates M. Fossa to the right. You quickly gain height up a steep flight of steps. The view sweeps round from Sicily with Mount Etna across Vulcano, Lipari, and Panarea to Strómboli. Cross the slope on the left. You come through dense undergrowth to a broad path which you walk along to the left, above the **Vallone del Castagno**. At the next fork continue to the right along the 'normal path'. The path soon heads downhill and then uphill again over some rock steps. For 1 hr. the path winds round numerous bends up through the dense wood

The old Hospiz Madonna del Terzito in the Valdichiesa.

as far as a forest road. First it swings to the left, then to the right to a fire-break. Paths lead into the wood opposite. The right-hand track goes via the forestry house to Valdichiesa. Continue the ascent across the firebreak to the left which leads past the bend of a road (take note of this for the return!) and up across two other roads to **Monte Fossa delle Felci**. Shortly before the summit cross go right and you have an excellent view of Valdichiesa, over to Monte Porri, and in the distance Filicudi and Alicudi.

Return along the firebreak as far as the bend of the return path. Now follow the lower road on the left-hand bend. On the ensuing right-hand bend take a narrow path on the left with wooden railings. Now descend round a lot of bends and cross the forest road twice. The second time continue along the road to the right (straight on is sign-posted to Leni) and go past two right-hand turn-offs. Watch out: 50 paces after the second turn-off leave the road to the left and zigzag down the narrow path.

With a view of the pilgrimage church you finally come down a few broad steps straight onto the road which leads left to the church of **Madonna del Terzito**. From here you reach the tarmac road and in a few minutes the bus stop on the main road.

47 Filicudi: Fossa Felci, 774m

No shade in the realm of the 'one covered in ferns'

Port – Valle Chiesa – Fossa Felci – Capo Graziano – port

Location: Filicudi Porto.
Starting point: port.
Walking times: port – Valle Chiesa 1 hr.,
Valle Chiesa – Fossa Felci 1 hr., Fossa
Felci – Valle Chiesa ¾ hr., Valle Chiesa –
Capo Graziano ¾ hr., Capo Graziano –
port ½ hr.; total time 4 hrs.
Ascent: 850m.
Grade: the path is unclear at times from
Valle Chiesa onwards. Good sense of

direction essential.
Food and accommodation: bars,
restaurants and hotels at the port, in the
area of Rocca di Ciaule and in Pecorini
Mare. For information see Walk 43.
Alternative: if you do not wish to climb up
to the summit, you can go straight on at
the wayside shrine in the big square in
Valle Chiesa and return along the mule
path to complete the round walk.

Filicudi lies at a more remote distance and is therefore quiet. Numerous
visitors are attracted here in the summer, especially by the archaeological
excavations at Capo Graziano. The slender rock needle of La Canna (reed),
also known as the 'walking stick of the Aeolians', is to be found in the west
where cliffs emerge in bizarre shapes from the deep-blue sea. The view
down from the summit of Fossa Felci is spectacular.

From the **port** a flight of steps leads up to the right and past the Pensione La
Canna straight on until it joins the tarmac road. Take the steps opposite to
the S. Stefano chapel and pass by on the left. Keep along the main path
where there are houses and shops. Later on the left there's a view of
Pecorini and you can see the tarmac road. A high stone wall runs off here on
the left. The broad path curves noticeably to the right and continues up
some wide steps to **Valle Chiesa**. When you arrive at the big square, go left

at a wayside shrine. At the second wayside shrine a few minutes later ascend right to Portella. At the last house (on the left there's an oven underneath a carob tree) you leave the path to the right and go steeply up a narrow flight of steps. Now zigzag up along a ridge in between rocks and macchia scrub. The ridge curves round to the left towards your destination which you can see from here. Eventually the path levels out a little and you reach the highest point of the **Fossa Felci** at a cairn. Continue westwards and at a rock spur you can see La Canna way down below (be careful!). The 'walking stick of the Aeolians' was first climbed by the Macugnaga members of the Italian Alpine Club. They discovered there a native population of white headed seagulls and an endemic species of lizard.

Return along the same path to the **Pensione La Canna** and turn right just afterwards. This path leads past a turn-off on the left down to the tarmac road. Walk left to the bend and on a path right ascend to the archaeological excavations at **Capo Graziano**. The foundations of round huts have been uncovered on two levels. A bit further over to the west you can look down onto the sea and also see the line of your walk. Back at the tarmac road, the path goes right to the **port.**

View of Capo Graziano with the archaeological excavations of the bronze Age village.

48 Alicudi: a round walk over steps

Uphill and downhill on heaven's ladders

Port – Chiesa del Carmine – Molino – port

Location: Mólo Nuovo.
Starting point: port in Alicudi.
Walking times: port – Chiesa d. Carmine ¼ hr., Chiesa d. Carmine – Molino ¾ hr., Molino – cemetery ½ hr., cemetery – port ¾ hr.; total time 2¼ hrs.
Ascent: 350m.
Grade: the flights of steps are rarely interrupted by flat sections. Hardly any waymarkers.
Food and accommodation: a hotel with the only bar/restaurant near to the port (June to September), otherwise rooms for rent where you can pre-order lunch. For information see Walk 43.

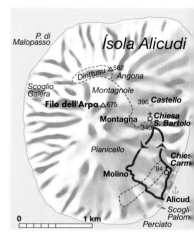

Alicudi, which originated 90,000 years ago, has a considerable height of over 2000m of which 600m is above the surface of the Tyrrhenian Sea. There are no beaches here, just steep cliffs which have little attraction for the tourist. There are no roads at all, instead thousands of steps ascend up to a height of 600m and criss-cross the island to link the settlements with one another. Donkeys and mules are used to carry loads. The charge is calculated according to the number of steps.

Go left from the **port** and turn right immediately under the fig tree, between the ferry office and the grocery shop, up the steps and past a turn-off on the left (the return path). Now stay on the broad path as far as a turn-off which leads over a ledge to the right. Go right here to reach the **Chiesa del Carmine**. The new Gothic church was built when more and more inhabitants from the upper settlements moved down to live closer to the port.

The path continues up past the church. Keep left on a flat section along the broad cobbled main path which again goes up some steps. After a ½ hr. ascent from the Chiesa del Carmine you reach a left hand turn-off. You can see the old church of San Bartolo up on the right. The main path climbs up to the church and then goes past it to the houses of Montagna, but you keep left at the turn-off. Past an ochre-coloured house with solar panels and another turn-off go up along the broad path. The view down to the left is of the port and the Chiesa del Carmine. There's a wayside shrine a little further on at the side of the path and an arrow indicates the way to Pianicello. From here the path is narrower, crosses the slope and on level ground leads past the first houses of **Molino** to a broad flight of steps on the right (sign-posted 'Eva Maria').

Watch out: go 35 paces left here down a narrow path to the next houses. Now some beautifully well-made steps wind down left round to the cemetery which you could see from above. Above it you come to a crosspath, go left, immediately right again and downhill. After the cemetery go down some more steps, past beautiful houses and orchards, to the **port**.

There's no use for bicycles in Alicudi.

49 Panarea: Punta del Corvo, 421m

Fancy walk on a posh island

Port – Punta del Corvo – Capo Milazzese/Cala Junco – port

Location: San Pietro.
Starting point: port in S. Pietro.
Walking times: port – P. d. Corvo 1½ hrs., P. d. Corvo – Cala Junco 1 hr., Cala Junco – port ¾ hr.; total time 3¼ hrs.
Ascent: 430m.
Grade: the first part of the summit slope is steep. The walk is marked red and white.
Food and accommodation: hotels and other accommodation in S. Pietro. See Walk 43.

The island has at its disposal a network of paths, marked and repaired to a high standard, which invites you to experience views down onto its wildly fissured west side and across to the group of islands in the east. An experience, so elegant, that the smart set of Panarea can only dream of it.

From the **port** go right, up the broad flight of steps and come to a road. Follow the signs to Calcara to the right. At the next turn-off the path leads straight on up to the Punta del Corvo. The marked path leads between villas and orchards gently ascending along a mule track to some cement steps. Waymarkers indicate right and a narrow path crosses the slope again. Behind a new building you come to the unsurfaced road which in due course joins the tarmac road. Go left here and up round some bends until you meet a mountain path on the left and some red and white waymarkers. Now begin the steep ascent up the slope. Very soon there are views down the right-hand side over the precipices to the deep-blue sea (be careful!). An island off an island, appropriately called Scoglio la Nave (ship of rocks), lies like a ship's keel at the foot of the rock faces. The path levels out after that. Isola Basiluzzo, the biggest rocky island belonging to the Panarea archipelago, can be seen from its most attractive side. Further along the marked path you come to **Punta del Corvo**. You can make out the shapes of Alicudi and Filicudi beyond the twin-peaked Salina. Lipari with its enormous dimensions and Vulcano can also be seen. On the descent you reach a turn-off. The path straight ahead goes directly to S. Pietro, but you go right southwards and descend at the edge of the steep cliffs and down some rock steps. Capo Milazzese is visible on the left with its archaeological excavations. 10 mins. from the summit you will see a conspicuous rock peak on the left, Castello. Go left at the next turn-off and cross the slope towards the peak: the path continues along a unmaintained stone wall (sometimes over rock steps) down to the plateau **Piano Milazzese**. Go left and reach the cobbled path. Right leads to the **Capo Milazzese/Cala Junco**, where archaeologists have discovered the foundations of some round huts dating from the 14th century BC. It's well worth making a detour to the site, not least because of the unique landscape of cliffs. Returning along the paved path, you first walk on the beach and then through the area of **Drauto** to S. Pietro and the **port**.

On the ascent to Punta del Corvo: Basiluzzo island and Strómboli.

50 Strómboli: Pizzo, 918m

The lighthouse from classical antiquity

Porto Scari – Labronzo – Pizzo – Rocazza – Semaforo San Vincenzo – Porto Scari

Locations: S. Vincenzo, S. Bartolo.
Starting point: Porto Scari (port).
Walking times: port – Labronzo 1 hr., Labronzo – Pizzo 2 hrs., Pizzo – Rocazza ½ hr., Rocazza – port 1 hr.; total time 4½ hrs.
Ascent: 950m.
Grade: obvious paths, sometimes marked. Steep sections with some easy scrambling on the ascent. The descent goes along an ash path. Be careful: if the wind is unfavourable unpleasant sulphur fumes can get into your eyes and lungs, and it can rain ash. High humidity can suddenly turn into mist and make route-finding difficult. For the descent at night do not neglect to check out the surrounding area at the viewpoint before darkness sets in, and a bit of the return path, too.

You are officially warned: 'only climb the crater in the company of authorised guides'.

Food and accommodation: big selection. For information see Walk 43.

NB: the office of the Cooperatività Strombolania can be found right at the port, tel: 090986390, fax: 090986396, e-mail: info@strombolania.it; their members are exceptionally helpful and offer every tourist service.

In 1930 almost the whole population left the island when a huge explosion devastated everything and there were ensuing sea quakes. Strómboli, the most active volcano in Europe, throws up molten rock and ash at regular intervals and is the scientific name for a type of volcano: the 'harmless ones' are the Strómboli volcanoes! Jules Verne's heroes emerge from Strómboli's crater in 'Journey to the Centre of the Earth'. The island was also the backdrop for Rosselini's film in 1950 where Ingrid Bergmann was moved to emotional outpourings.

From the **port** go up the narrow street next to the ferry office to the Piazza of **S. Vincenzo**. Just before the square on the left there is a little road with a waymarker. This is where you return. Past the church go left as far as the next cross-road. Go left here round an S-bend. Now the road gently descends to S. Bartolo. Past the church you come to the houses of Piscità. At the following left-hand turn-off with big signposts, follow the 'Via Domenico Cincota' to the left. The little road goes through Piscità, gets narrower and then goes uphill. Shortly after **Labronzo** you reach the turn-off right to the 'Pizzeria l'Osservatorio' from where you can look up to the crater. Go left through some tall reeds and round long zigzags to the end of the cobbled path. There's a good view of Sciara del Fuoco here and you can hear and smell the volcano. From here descend along a steep white, sometimes red marked path, and in places scramble up a solidified lava flow to reach the ridge. The now sandy path levels out and goes past small tiered walls, where many people set up their camp for the night. With views to the craters to the right, the path curves round along the ridge up to the **Pizzo**. Past measuring instruments and the return path (on the left) you come leisurely downhill to the Strómboli 'viewing balcony' where you can look across all the craters. Be careful! For the return, first go back to the Pizzo from the viewpoint, descend to the right and to the Portella le Croci. Then the de-

Semaforo Labronzo
115
Piscitá
S. Bartolo
31
Ficogrande
S. Vincenzo
Scari
195
Semaforo
S. Vincenzo
'sola di Strómboli
Sciara del Fuoco
Crateri
Pizzo o Sopra la Fossa △
918
Le Croci
Rocazza
△ **I Vancori**
924
Malpasseddu
Ginostra
△
Frontone
853
Malpasso
Secche di Lazzaro
Malo Passo
P. dell'Omo
La Lena
P. Lena
0   1 km

A view of the S. Vincenzo area as you arrive on the island.

scent begins along the ash track. The port lies far below and in the same direction in the black sand you can see a large porphyry-red rock below with an arrow – **Rocazza**.

Keep left at the rock and after a few brief ascents, continue through a landscape of reeds. You pass telephone aerials and the Semaforo S. Vincenzo as you gradually approach S. Vincenzo along some roadways. When you reach the Piazza return to the **port** to the right.

Waiting for darkness on the Pizzo, 918m, to experience the interior of the earth.

Index